KT-561-698

Welcome to Dubai

Dubai is gearing up to host World Expo 2020, but clued-in travellers know that this tiny powerhouse emirate has long been an exciting place for foodies, fun seekers, shoppers, art lovers and desert rats to visit. Whether you're looking for the simple life or futuristic luxury, you'll be sure to find it in this peaceful outpost brimming with energy, optimism and openness.

Dubai Marina (p123)
ASHRAF JANDALI/SHUTTERSTOCK ©

Top Sights

Burj Khalifa

This architectural stunner is the world's tallest building. **p104**

LUCIANO MORTULA - LGM/SHUTTERSTOCK ©

Al Fahidi Historic District

In the footsteps of Old Dubai. **p52**

Dubai Museum

Dubai history in a nutshell. **p50**

Burj Al Arab

Iconic symbol of modern Dubai. **p88**

Gold Souq
Strolling the City of Gold. **p32**

MELIS/SHUTTERSTOCK ©

BUENA VISTA IMAGES/GETTY IMAGES ©

Dubai Mall
The mother of all malls. **p106**

Madinat Jumeirah

Twenty-first-century Arabian village rebooted. **p86**

R.A.R. DE BRUIJN HOLDING BV/SHUTTERSTOCK ©

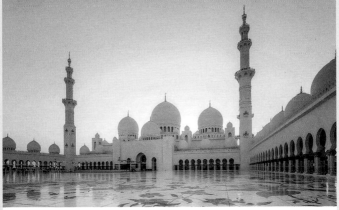

BOULE/SHUTTERSTOCK ©

Abu Dhabi

Capital of art and culture. **p142**

Eating

Dining in Dubai is an extraordinarily multicultural experience. Arabic and Indian fare are the most prevalent, but you can feast on anything from kebabs to fish and chips in the city's myriad eateries. These run the gamut from simple street kitchens to luxe dining temples.

Farm to Fork

Taking global fare local is not unique to Dubai, but it's arrived with a vengeance. As awareness has grown, demand for certified organic produce has increased right along with it. Farms in the UAE have expanded their operations, and farmers markets pop up all over. Even supermarkets have joined the locavore trend by marking the origin of their produce.

Emirati Cuisine

Restaurants serving Emirati food used to be rare, but thankfully this is changing. Typical dishes are one-pot stews featuring a combination of grains, vegetables and meat or fish, flavoured with spices and topped with nuts or dried fruit.

Camel Milk

Known to Bedouin for centuries, the health benefits of camel milk have caught international attention. Slightly pungent and salty in taste, it's lower in fat and more vitamin-rich than cow's milk. Restaurants have also started to put camel dishes on their menus, although it's not traditionally an Emirati staple.

Best Cheap Eats

Ravi Empty tables are as rare as hen's teeth at this unfussy curry temple with sidewalk seating. (p78)

Al Ustad Special Kabab Sheiks to shoe shiners fill this cool been-here-forever Iranian kebab joint. (p62)

Al Tawasol Sit on the floor Bedouin-style for a cutlery-free classic Yemeni feast. (p42)

JOSHUA GM/SHUTTERSTOCK ©

Best Emirati Food

Logma Casual cafe that serves modern Emirati cuisine from breakfast to dessert. (p77)

Aseelah Successfully bridges traditional and contemporary Emirati food and decor. (p41)

Al Fanar This traditional spot is an ode to Emirati culinary heritage. (p79)

Best Middle Eastern

Qwaider Al Nabulsi Makes fluffy falafel and some of the best *kunafa* (pictured; vermicelli-like pastry soaked in syrup) in town. (p42)

Zaroob Lebanese street-food staples in an urban indoor setting. (p113)

Best Indian

Indego by Vineet Michelin man Vineet Bhatia seduces diners with contemporary spins on Indian classics. (p133)

Eric's Unassuming neigh-bourhood charmer delivers a taste-bud tingling culinary journey to Goa. (p62)

Sind Punjab Spicy budget curries are the currency at one of Dubai's oldest Indian eateries. (p62)

Best Vegetarian

Saravana Dhavan Don't let the unassuming decor put you off – the all-veg Indian food is tops. (p63)

Govinda's Serves Sattvic food that not only eschews meat but also oil, onion and garlic. (p64)

Top Tips

Make weekend bookings, including Friday brunch, for top tables at least a week ahead. Note that only licensed hotel restaurants and independent venues may serve alcohol.

Bars

Dubai may be famous for glam clubs, but it's also developing a more low-key underground scene. Dubai's weekend nights (Thursday and Friday) are busiest, when party animals let off steam in bars and on the dance floor. Alcohol is served in hotels and some licensed venues only.

Bars & Pubs

Venues in Downtown Dubai, Jumeirah, Dubai Marina and Palm Jumeirah tend to appeal mostly to well-heeled visitors and expats. Beachfront lounges and rooftop bars continue to be popular. Bars and pubs in Bur Dubai and Deira are more low-key, gritty affairs. Note that prostitution, though officially illegal, is tolerated in many establishments.

Shisha & Mocktails

Most Emiratis don't drink alcohol, preferring to socialise over coffee, juice and mocktails. Join them in a mellow shisha cafe and sample a puff to better understand this Middle Eastern pastime.

Happy Hours & Ladies' Nights

Take advantage of happy hours offered by most bars, from dives to five-star lounges. Many go to great lengths to lure women with free cocktails, bubbly and nibbles, especially on Tuesdays and Wednesday.

Best Beachfront Bars

Jetty Lounge Sip artful potions while tucked into an overstuffed sofa at this sensuously styled bar. (p137)

Bliss Lounge Chilled Dubai Marina dispensary of some of the finest cocktails in town. (p137)

Zero Gravity Bustling beach club with restaurant and bar. (p141)

Best Rooftop Bars

Siddharta Lounge Cocktails with a view of the glittering Dubai Marina at this ab-fab lounge by the pool. (p137)

40 Kong Power players loosen their ties and inhibitions at this swank outdoor bar. (p118)

RUS S/SHUTTERSTOCK ©

Treehouse Cocktails with views of Burj Khalifa in posh living-room-style cosiness. (p117)

Best for Happy Hours & Ladies' Nights

Pure Sky Lounge Sunsets over the Gulf go well with half-price drinks daily between 5pm and 7pm. (p137)

Bahri Bar Three free glasses of bubbly in this Arabian-styled bar with Burj Al Arab views. (p98)

Lucky Voice Buy one, get one free every day from 4pm to 8pm. (p136)

Barasti Beachfront institution; 30% drink discounts daily, plus bottomless sparkly for women on Tuesdays. (p135)

Best Pubs

Irish Village The classic (pictured) is still going strong after nearly 20 years in business. (p44)

Fibber Magee's A bit down at the heel, but that just adds to the character of this perennial pub fave. (p118)

George & Dragon Channel your inner Bukowski at this hardcore barfly hangout. (p65)

Best for Shisha & Mocktails

Reem Al Bawadi Spin tales of romance and adventure while kicking back in this Dubai Marina spot. (p125)

QDs Puff away languidly while looking out on the shimmering Creek and skyline. (p45)

Top Tips

Dubai has zero-tolerance laws on drink driving. Getting caught could entail fines or jail time. Note, too, that since 2016, Dubai bars are also open – and serve alcohol – during Ramadan. Most clubs close during this period.

Shopping

Shopping is a favourite pastime in Dubai, which boasts not only the world's largest mall but also shopping centres that resemble ancient Egypt or an Italian village and feature ski slopes, ice rinks and giant aquariums. Souqs provide more traditional flair, and a growing crop of urban outdoor malls, indie boutiques and galleries beckon as well.

Trends

Recently, urban outdoor malls have arrived, like BoxPark in Jumeirah and City Walk near Downtown Dubai, which have a carefully curated smaller number of stores. There's also a growing crop of indie designer boutiques as well as thriving flea markets.

Bargaining Basics

Prices in malls and most stores are fixed, but in souqs and outdoor markets it pays to know some bargaining basics. A good rule of thumb is to cut the first suggested price in half and go from there. Expect to finish up with a discount of 20% to 30%. If you intend to buy more than one item, use this as a bargaining chip. For more, see A Primer on Bargaining (p47).

Carpet Buying

Dubai has a reputation in the region for having the highest-quality carpets at the best prices. Fine Persian carpets, colourful Turkish and Kurdish kilims and rough-knotted Bedouin rugs are all widely available. Bargaining is the norm. If buying, be sure to ask for a Certificate of Authentication issued by the Dubai Chamber of Commerce & Industry.

Best Shopping Malls

Dubai Mall A power shopper's Shangri-La, Dubai Mall is the largest shopping mall in the world. (p106)

Mall of the Emirates Get lost amid the ample temptations of this mega-mall famous for its indoor ski slope. (p100)

BoxPark This urban strip brims with cool cafes and eclectic boutiques in shipping containers. (p82)

Best Markets

Ripe Market Happening market in Zabeel Park with quality local produce, handmade art and craft and international food stalls. (p67)

Dubai Flea Market Bargains abound at this monthly market on the beautiful grounds of Zabeel Park. (p67)

Best for Indie Fashion

S*uce Home-grown concept store showcases regional designers in fashion, accessories and jewellery. (p82)

O Concept This edgy Jumeirah boutique has young things looking good at reasonable price tags. (p82)

Best Modern Souqs

Souk Al Bahar Across from Dubai Mall, this richly decorated Arabesque souq teems with restaurants and souvenir stores. (p121)

Souk Madinat Jumeirah This tourist-geared souq follows a harmonious rhythm of courtyards, alleyways and outdoor areas. (p87)

Best for Gifts & Souvenirs

Bateel Delicious dates presented like precious jewels in an elegant boutique setting. (p67)

Mirzam Dubai's own chocolate factory wraps its yummy single-origin bean bars in artistic designs. (p91)

Jalabiyat Yasmine Fabulous assortment of quality pashminas, including precious hand-embroidered ones. (p100)

For Kids

Travelling to Dubai with kids can be child's play. There's plenty to do – from water parks and playgrounds to theme parks and activity centres. Most beach resorts operate kids' clubs, giving you ample peace to work on your tan or skip off to the spa.

Junior Foodies

Kids are welcome at all but the most formal restaurants, although you might feel more relaxed at casual spots. All malls boast extensive food courts, and hotels have at least one restaurant suitable for families. There's also a growing crop of kid-geared cafes, including BookMunch Cafe (p98).

Playgrounds & Parks

Dubai has a handful of parks with picnic areas and playgrounds for children to let off steam (just don't go in the searing heat of July and August). One of the biggest and best for activities is Zabeel Park (pictured; p60), home of the new Dubai Frame (p59).

Teen Time

OK, so they've done the ski slopes, disco-danced at the ice rink, splashed around at the water parks and enjoyed a fashionable strut around the malls. Is there more to prevent teens from succumbing to boredom? To impress their pals back home, consider taking them sandboarding, camel riding on an overnight desert safari or even a trekking trip to the Hajar Mountains.

Best Water Parks

Aquaventure Waterpark One of the largest water parks in the world with lots of rides for thrill junkies. (p128)

Wild Wadi Waterpark Family favourite with attractions ranging from gentle pools to kamikaze slides. (p95)

Best Theme Parks

IMG Worlds of Adventure Thrill rides with dinos, superheroes and cartoon characters in the world's largest indoor amusement

PELIKH ALEXEY/SHUTTERSTOCK ©

park. (www.imgworlds.com; adult/child under 1.2m/child under 1.05m Dhs245/225/ free)

Motiongate Indoor-outdoor park counts rides inspired by *Ghostbusters*, *Shrek* and *The Hunger Games* among its attractions. (www.motion gatedubai.com; adult/child Dhs330/280)

Hub Zero Gamers make a beeline to this indoor theme park for a VR immersion, race simulators and laser tag battles. (p75)

Best for Animal Attractions

Dubai Aquarium & Underwater Zoo Kids will be mesmerised by the sharks, groupers and rays flitting about this giant three-storey aquarium in Dubai Mall. (p107)

Lost Chambers Aquarium For another audience with fishy friends, head to this labyrinth of underwater tanks and tunnels teeming with exotic denizens at Atlantis The Palm. (p129)

Green Planet This indoor rainforest brings the tropics to the desert, complete with birds, frogs, lizards, butterflies, turtles and other critters. (p75)

Best for Chilled-out Kids

Dubai Ice Rink Tots to teens can cool down with pirouettes and disco dancing at Dubai Mall's ice rink. (p110)

Ski Dubai Alpine slopes, toboggan tracks and penguin encounters await at this massive indoor winter wonderland. (p95)

Top Tips

Many hotels have kids clubs and child-care centres. For babysitting, ask for a referral at your hotel or try www.dubaimetromaids. com or www.maidszone.com. Note, too, in Dubai, children under five travel free on public transport.

Clubbing

DJs spin every night of the week with the top names hitting the decks on Thursdays and Fridays. Partying is not restricted to nighttime; plenty of beach clubs open at midday on weekends in the cooler months. The sound repertoire is global – funk, soul, trip-hop, hip-hop, R&B, African, Arabic and Latino – although the emphasis is still clearly on house, tech and other EDM.

Global DJs

Globetrotting big-name DJs like Ellen Allien, Carl Craig, Steve Aoki, Russ Yallop, Roger Sanchez and Ben Klock occasionally jet in for the weekend to whip the crowd into a frenzy in the top venues and at mega-parties like Groove on the Grass or Party in the Park. But there's plenty of resident spin talent as well. The roster is constantly in flux, of course, but names to keep on the radar include Jixo & Danz, KayteK, Siamak Amidi, Hoolz, Scott Forshaw, Ron E Jazz and Josephine De Retour.

Parties

Some top parties are put on by local record labels, promoters or event agencies such as Audio Tonic (progressive house), Plus Minus (deep house and techno), Analog Room (underground techno-electro), Stereo Club (electro), Globalfunk (drum & bass), Superheroes (house, drum & bass), Bassworx (drum & bass) and Bad House Party (indie-punk-eclectic).

Best for Top DJs

Cirque Le Soir Flamboyant circus-themed club for uninhibited partying. (p117)

White Dubai Megaclub with dizzying light show on top of the Meydan Racecourse. (p120)

Base State-of-the-art partying in this giant club in Dubai Design District. (p117)

Best for Outdoor Partying

Barasti Any time is a good time to stumble into the original party village in the sand. (p135)

Zero Gravity Bustling beach club with restaurant and bar. (p141)

360° Watch the sun drop behind the Burj Al Arab at

DARYL VISSCHER/GETTY IMAGES ©

this sizzling offshore party den. (p98)

White Dubai Beirut import above the Meydan horse track in a glitterati fave. (p120)

Best for Underground Vibes

Industrial Avenue Warehouse-style hidden club with graffiti and nonmainstream electro. (p137)

Casa Latina Unpretentious Cuban-themed bar that hosts wicked parties. (p99)

Best Glam Factor

Club Boudoir Swish venue for beautiful people gyrating

to a sound mix from hip-hop to desi (Bollywood). (p81)

Cavalli Club Bling brigadiers should strap on those heels and make a beeline for this sparkling dancing den. (p118)

Cirque Le Soir Acrobats, jugglers and clowns make this cabaret-style nightclub a superhot ticket. (p117)

Top Tips

Keep tabs on club news with the free biweekly *Hype* magazine, available at bars, boutiques, gyms and spas and on www. magster.com. Other listings include www. infusion.ae, www.platinumlist.ae, www. residentadvisor.net and www.timeout.com

Art

Fueled by artists from around the world, Dubai's art scene has become one of the most dynamic in the Gulf region. Art aficionados will find their compass on perpetual spin with a growing number of galleries, private collections, street art and high-profile art events.

IMAGE COURTESY ALSERKAL AVENUE ©

Gallery Quarters

Galleries in Dubai cluster in two main areas: emerging, underground and experimental art in the Alserkal Avenue campus (pictured) in industrial Al Quoz, and more established contenders in Gate Village. Dubai art-world pioneers cluster around Bur Dubai's Al Fahidi Historic District.

Urban & Street Art

Dubai's urban art scene has developed thanks to the Dubai Street Museum project. Large-scale murals celebrating the UAE's history decorate 2nd December St in Satwa, and funky creations line City Walk in Jumeirah. Artful graffiti is also scattered around the Al Fahidi Historic District in Bur Dubai.

Dubai Art Week

Held in March, Dubai Art Week centres on Art Dubai (www.art-dubai.ae), a gathering of nearly 100 galleries from the UAE and abroad at Madinat Jumeirah. There's also Design Days Dubai and the Sikka Art Fair (www.sikka.ae), for which local artists create site-specific works in the Al Fahidi Historic District.

Best for Middle Eastern Art

Ayyam Gallery This top international gallery has branches in both Alserkal Avenue and Gate Village. (p110)

The Third Line Represents top regional artists here and at international art fairs. (p91)

Leila Heller Gallery Art-world top dogs and promising up-and-comers. (p91)

Gallery Isabelle van den Eynde Shepherds regional emerging and midcareer artists to prominence. (p91)

Tours

STEVE LOVEGROVE/SHUTTERSTOCK ©

If you're a Dubai first-timer, letting someone else show you around is a fun and efficient way to get your bearings, see the key sights quickly and obtain a general understanding of the city. All manner of exploration – from city bus tours to mosque visits – is available.

Dubai in Depth

Dubai offers a growing number of guided explorations to match all sorts of interests. Take a classic bus tour if you just want to get an introduction to the city or join a themed walking tour for an in-depth look at certain facets of daily life. The Sheikh Mohammed Centre for Cultural Understanding offers the best tours for an introduction to Emirati culture. They're the only ones who take non-Muslims inside a mosque and also offer breakfasts and lunches where you can taste the local cuisine. Hardcore foodies should go on Frying Pan Adventures for a mouthwatering immersion in Dubai street food culture.

Best Walking Tours

Al Fahidi Historic District Peel back the curtain on Dubai's past on a tour with the Sheikh Mohammed Centre for Cultural Understanding. (p58)

Frying Pan Adventures Plunge headlong into the culinary labyrinth of multicultural Bur Dubai and Deira on these fun and educational guided food tours. (p64)

Jumeirah Mosque The only mosque in Dubai (pictured) that can be visited by non-Muslims; guided tours offered daily except Friday. (p74)

Best Bus Tours

Big Bus Dubai Hop-on, hop-off tours with commentary in 12 languages linking Dubai's major sights and landmarks on three interconnecting routes. (p61)

Wonder Bus Tours Discover Dubai's historic centre on one-hour land and water tours aboard an ingenious amphibious bus. (p77)

Best Boat Tours

Dubai Ferry Value-priced minicruises let you appreciate the city skyline from the water. (p66)

Al Mansour Dhow Float past the glittering Creek lights while indulging in a buffet dinner on a historic dhow. (p43)

Four Perfect Days

Day 1

CHUBIS/SHUTTERSTOCK ©

Day 2

PLAMEN GALABOV/SHUTTERSTOCK ©

Follow our **Bur Dubai Waterside Walk** through the **Al Fahidi** (p55) and **Shindagha** (p59) historic districts. Hop on the ferry to Deira to peruse the dazzling **Spice** (p38), **Gold** (p35) and **Perfume** (p38) souqs, then board the metro at Palm Deira station.

Catapult into the future in Downtown Dubai. Head to massive **Dubai Mall** (p106), with 1200 stores plus **Dubai Aquarium** (p107) and an **ice rink** (p110). It's dwarfed by the sky-piercing **Burj Khalifa** (p104); book for a sunset ascent.

Coming down, admire the **Dubai Fountain** (p107), take a taxi to Madinat Jumeirah for dinner with Burj Al Arab views at **Pierchic** (p96), then finish with quiet drinks at **Bahri Bar** (p98).

Join the guided tour of the gorgeous **Jumeirah Mosque** (p74), the only one in Dubai open to non-Muslims, then walk over to the **Etihad Museum** (p74) to learn the founding of the UAE.

Try traditional Emirati lunch at **Al Fanar** (p79), then relax on the sands for a couple of hours on **Kite** (pictured; p94) or **JBR** (p129) beach.

Rinse off the salt for happy hour cocktails at **Bliss Lounge** (p137) or **Pure Sky Lounge** (p137). For dinner, decide between views of the Gulf at **Indego by Vineet** (p133) or the yachts in the marina at **Asia Asia** (p141). Wind down the night in style on the breezy terrace of **Siddharta Lounge** (p137).

Day 3

FOKKE BAARSSEN/SHUTTERSTOCK ©

Day 4

JIANG_LIU/SHUTTERSTOCK ©

Start with a healthy breakfast at ultrahip **Tom & Serg** (p91), then a gallery hop around the **Alserkal Avenue** (p90) warehouse complex.

Get a taxi to the **Mall of the Emirates** (p100) to see **Ski Dubai** (pictured; p95), and spend the afternoon keeping cool here or getting wet at the **Wild Wadi Waterpark** (p95). Pop back to Madinat Jumeirah to pick up **souq** (p87) souvenirs and take an **abra tour** (p87) of the resort's canal network.

Located at the end of a long pier, **360°** (p98) is the best sundowner spot with the Burj Al Arab as a backdrop. Reserve for dinner at **101 Lounge & Bar** (p133) to marvel at the twinkling skyscrapers while you dine. Get there by free shuttle from the **One&Only Royal Mirage** (p147).

It's time to sample desert serenity on the authentic Bedouin Culture Safari with **Platinum Heritage Tours** (p130). It includes a camel ride to a desert camp where you join Bedu for breakfast and meet their hunting dogs and falcons. You'll be back in town around noon.

IMG Worlds of Adventure (p16) is the world's largest indoor theme park. It's filled with fun and thrilling rides, and an afternoon spent here passes in no time.

For dinner, head to The Walk at JBR for scrumptious Italian fare at **BiCE** (p135), then finish with a stroll along **The Beach at JBR** (p128) with a view of the **Ain Dubai** (p128) Ferris wheel.

Need to Know

For detailed information, see Survival Guide p145

Currency
Dirham (Dhs)

Languages
Arabic, English, Urdu

Visas
Citizens of 49 countries, including all EU countries, the US, the UK, Canada and Australia, are eligible for free 30-day single-entry visas on arrival in Dubai.

Money
ATMs are widely available. Credit cards are accepted in most hotels, restaurants and shops.

Mobile Phones
Mobile phones operate on GSM900/1800. Local SIM cards are easy to find in electronics stores and some grocery stores.

Time
Dubai is four hours ahead of GMT. No daylight savings.

Daily Budget

Budget: Less than Dhs600
Budget hotel room: Dhs300–400
Meal in a food court: Dhs20-50
Public transport: Dhs1-8.50

Midrange: Dhs600–1200
Double room in a hotel: Dhs400–700
Two-course meal without alcohol in a restaurant: from Dhs80
Entry to top attractions and sights: Dhs100-200

Top end: More than Dhs1200
Four-star hotel room: from Dhs800
Three-course fine-dining meal with wine: from Dhs400
Drinks in a high-end bar: from Dhs100

Advance Planning

Three months or more before Double-check visa regulations. Book tickets for high-profile sporting and entertainment events.

One month before Reserve a table at top restaurants, tickets for Burj Khalifa and golf tee-times. Check concert venue websites for what's on during your stay.

One week before Check average daytime temperature and pack accordingly.

Arriving in Dubai

Taxis and the Dubai metro are both convenient modes of transport to/from the airport. Note that cabbies navigate not by addresses but by landmarks (such as malls, big hotels, beaches).

✈ Dubai International Airport

Metro Red Line runs every few minutes between 6am and midnight, from terminals 1 and 3.

Bus Buses takes over from Metro from midnight to 6am.

Taxis Flag fall of Dhs25; Dhs50 to Deira, Dhs80 to Downtown Dubai.

✈ From Al Maktoum International Airport

Bus F55 goes to Ibn Battuta metro station to connect to Dubai Metro Red Line.

Taxis Around Dhs70 to Dubai Marina and Dhs110 to Downtown Dubai.

Getting Around

The Dubai metro is an inexpensive, speedy and comfortable mode of transport. Buses offer good coverage but are slow and have baffling timetables. Before using public transport, you must purchase a rechargeable pass (Nol card; www.nol.ae) from ticket offices or vending machines.

🚇 Metro

Red and Green Lines link all major sights and neighbourhoods, runs 5.30am and midnight Saturday to Wednesday, and to 1am Thursday and Friday (from 10am on Friday).

🚕 Taxi

Taxis are metered, air-conditioned and the fastest and most comfortable way to get around, except during rush hour. Hail in the street, at taxi ranks or book by phone and the free Smart Taxi App.

🚗 Uber & Careem

Ride-hailing apps such as Uber (www.uber.com) and Dubai based Careem (www.careem.com).

🚌 Bus

Fairly slow, but clean and useful for stops not served by the metro.

⛴ Boat

Abras (traditional wooden ferries) cross the Creek between Deira and Bur Dubai. The Dubai Ferry operates on two interlinking routes along the Dubai Canal and between Bur Dubai and Dubai Marina.

🚊 Tram

The Dubai Tram travels along King Salman Bin Abdul Aziz Al Saud St between Dubai Media City and Dubai Marina.

Dubai Neighbourhoods

Dubai Marina & Palm Jumeirah (p123)
Tailor-made for hedonists, this area entices with beaches, luxury hotels, a pedestrian-friendly marina and sizzling nightlife.

Burj Al Arab

👁 👁

Madinat Jumeirah

Burj Al Arab & Madinat Jumeirah (p85)
A modern Arabian village with superb beaches, restaurants and souvenir shopping, backed by the iconic Burj Al Arab.

Abu Dhabi (p142)
This city has built up an impressive portfolio of breathtaking attractions, including the stunning Sheik Zayed Grand Mosque, and the new Louvre Abu Dhabi.

Jumeirah & Around (p71)

Hugging a fabulous stretch of beach, this villa-studded residential area also has plenty in store for fashionistas and adventurous foodies.

Bur Dubai (p49)

Dubai's historic hub is a polycultural potpourri of restored buildings, budget eateries, shopping bargains and photogenic Creek views.

Dubai Museum

Gold Souq

Al Fahidi Historic District

Burj Khalifa

Dubai Mall

Dubai International Airport

Deira (p31)

Charismatic, crowded and cacophonous, Deira's twisting roads are loaded with atmospheric souqs, heritage sites and fantastic eats.

Downtown Dubai (p103)

The Burj Khalifa presides over the city's futuristic centre with plenty to delight shoppers, families and art and architecture fans alike.

Explore
Dubai

Worth a Trip 🔭

Dubai's Walking Tours 🥾

Dubai Experience 🍽️

Desert camel ride with view of Dubai BUENA VISTA IMAGES/GETTY IMAGES ©

Explore

Deira

Hugging the northern side of the Creek, Deira is one of Dubai's oldest and most charismatic neighbourhoods. Dusty, crowded and chaotic, it feels world away from the slick new districts along Sheikh Zayed Rd. Along the Creek, colourful wooden dhows plough their trade between Iran, Sudan and other locales. Nearby, the bustling souqs are ancestors to today's malls, where you can sip tea and haggle for bargains with traders tending generations-old stores.

The most historic area is Al Ras, near the mouth of the Creek, home to century-old pearl traders' homes and the city's first school, but Deira's most seductive lure is its cluster of atmospheric souqs. This tangle of narrow lanes heaves with a cacophony of sounds and smells that bursts to life in the morning and late afternoon.

Deira is also Dubai's most multicultural neighbour-hood, peacefully shared by immigrants from around the globe. Many operate restaurants serving authentic fare from places such as India, Syria, Lebanon, Ethiopia, Iraq and Afghanistan. Alternatively, book a dinner cruise aboard a festively decorated dhow, or head to a Creekside alfresco lounge in a high-end hotel.

Getting There & Around

The main sights of Deira are all within easy walking distance of each other around the mouth of Dubai Creek.

Ⓜ Red and Green Lines, intersect at Union station

⛴ Abras link the souqs in Deira and Bur Dubai across the Creek.

Deira Map on p36

Spices for sale in the Spice Souq (p38) FEDOR SELIVANOV/SHUTTERSTOCK ©

Top Sight

Gold Souq

*'Dubai: City of Gold' screams the banner atop
the LED display at the towering entrance gate to
Dubai's Gold Souq; you'll feel as though you've
just plunged into a latter-day Aladdin's cave.
Lining a wooden-latticed central arcade and
spidery lanes are hundreds of shops spilling over
with gold, diamonds, pearls, silver and platinum.
It's a dazzling display, from simple rings to
intricate wedding necklaces, and a must-see.*

◎ MAP P36, B2

Sikkat al Khail St

🕙 10am-1pm & 3-10pm

Ⓜ Al Ras

The Real Deal?

No need to worry about fakes at the Gold Souq. The quality of gold is government-regulated, so you can be fairly confident that the piece of jewellery you've got your eye on is genuine (unlike the Rolex watches or Prada bags touts are trying to tempt you with). Price is determined by weight based on the official daily international rate and on the artistry of the item. Haggling is expected and vendors build in price buffers accordingly. Sharp bargaining skills usually make merchants drop the initial asking price by 20% to 30%. The price of gold itself is fixed, so focus on the intricacy of the artisanship as a point of discussion.

Record-Breaking Gold Ring

Dubai being the capital of superlatives, the Gold Souq is naturally home to a record-breaking piece of jewellery. Stop at the Kanz shop just past the main souq entrance (off Old Baladiya St) to snap a selfie with the world's largest and heaviest gold ring, as certified by none other than Guinness World Records. Called the Najmat Taiba (Star of Taiba), the 21-carat beauty weighs in at nearly 64kg and is worth a hefty US$3 million.

People-Watching

Simply watching the goings-on at the souq is another treat, especially during the bustling evenings. Settle down on a bench, buy a bottle of juice from one of the itinerant sellers and take in the colourful street theatre. With a little patience, you should see hard-working Afghan men dragging heavy carts of goods, African women in bright kaftans balancing their purchases on their heads, and chattering local women out on a shopping spree.

★ Top Tips

o The best time to visit is in the bustling evenings; mornings are busy with tour groups and afternoons sleepy.

o Credit cards are almost always accepted, but you'll get a better price with cash.

o If you don't see anything you like, don't panic. Most shops will make something to your own design.

o Don't rush! Remember, you don't have to make a decision on the spot. Compare carefully before you buy and be prepared to haggle.

✖ Take a Break

A classic pit stop in these parts is **Ashwaq** (cnr Al Soor & Sikkat al Khail Sts; sandwiches Dhs4-7; ⊙8.30am-midnight; Ⓜ Palm Deira), whose shawarma rocks the palate. Wash it down with a freshly squeezed fruit juice.

Walking Tour 🚶

Deira Souq Stroll

The Deira souq area is one of the most historic and atmospheric districts in Dubai and is best explored by foot. It's a bustling, nicely chaotic warren of lanes teeming with exotic stalls and shops and especially bustling in the evenings. This tour covers the main bazaars and also incorporates a couple of heritage stops into its route.

Walk Facts

Start Deira Old Souq abra station

End Afghan Khorasan Kebab

Length 2km; three hours

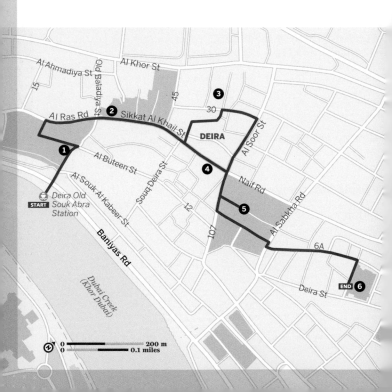

❶ Spice Souq

As soon as you step off the abra at Deira Old Souq abra station, heady scents will lure you across to the **Spice Souq** (p38). Follow your nose around to find saffron, turmeric, frankincense and more. To learn about one of Dubai's finest poets, pop into the **Museum of the Poet Al Oqaili** (p39).

❷ Gold Souq

Find your way to Al Ras Rd and turn right to Old Baladiya St. Find the wooden latticed entrance gate of the **Gold Souq** (p32), easily recognised by the lettering 'City of Gold'. Take a selfie with the world's largest gold ring, then peruse the bling displayed in dozens of shop windows, from petite earrings to over-the-top gold pieces created for bridal dowries.

❸ Women's Museum

Head north of the central arcade to suss out tiny teashops, cafeterias, busy tailors and barber shops lining narrow lanes. Look for signs pointing the way to the **Women's Museum** (p39) to learn about the important contributions made by Emirati women in such fields as art, science and education.

❹ Perfume Souq

Head back south and turn left onto 32a St, then follow it to Al Soor St and one of the main drags of the **Perfume Souq** (p38). Turn right and sniff out pungent Arabian *attars* (perfume oil) and *oud* (fragrant wood oil), then grab a juice or schwarma at **Ashwaq Cafeteria** (p33) at the corner with Sikkat al Khail Rd.

❺ Covered Souq

Cut diagonally across the intersection and plunge into the tiny alleys of the **Covered Souq** (p40), where you'll find shops selling everything from textiles to sheesha pipes. It's fun to explore, watch the crowd haggle for deals, and perhaps even ferret out your own bargain.

❻ Naif Market

Find your way to Al Sabkha Rd and head down 6A St to get to the **Naif Market** (p40), on the site of the historic Naif Souq. Wrap up with a carnivorous feast at **Afghan Khorasan Kabab** (p44), in an adjacent alley next to the Al Ghurair Mosque.

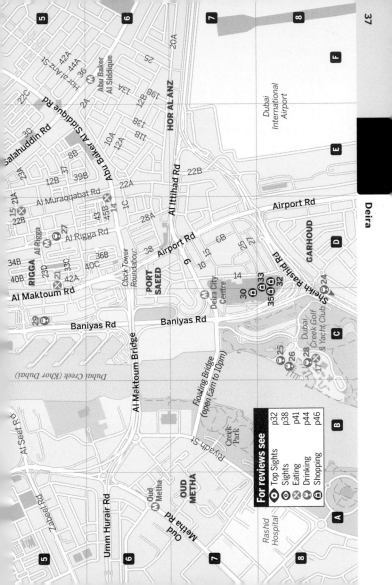

Deira

5

6

7

8

Hor al Anz St

42A

44A

36

Abu Baker
Al Siddique

22C

Rd

Salahuddin Rd

30

23A

8B

37

12B

39B

Al Muraqqabat Rd

15 21A

22B

27

43

45B

14

Al Rigga

Al Rigga Rd

34B

40B

23D

21

36B

40C

42A

Al Maktoum Rd

29

Baniyas Rd

Dubai Creek (Khor Dubai)

Al Maktoum Bridge

Al Seef Rd

Zabeel Rd

Umm Hurair Rd

Abu Baker Al Siddique Rd

HOR AL ANZ

20A

25

13A

19B

12B

13B

10A

11B

12A

22A

1C

28A

Al Ittihad Rd

22B

Airport Rd

6

6B

28

Clock Tower
Roundabout

PORT
SAEED

Baniyas Rd

Floating Bridge
(open 6am to 10pm)

Riyadh St

Creek
Park

OUD
METHA

Oud
Metha

Oud Metha Rd

Rashid
Hospital

Airport Rd

GARHOUD

10

15

6B

25

27

Sheikh Rashid Rd

24

14

33

30

35

32

Deira City
Centre

Dubai
Creek Golf
& Yacht Club

25

26

28

17

Dubai
International
Airport

For reviews see

Top Sights   p32
Sights   p38
Eating   p41
Drinking   p44
Shopping   p46

A   B   C   D   E   F

5

6

7

8

Dubai Creek

What the Tiber is to Rome and the Thames is to London, the Creek is to Dubai: a defining stretch of water at the heart of the city. Known as Al Khor in Arabic, the Creek was the base of local fishing and pearling industries in the early 20th century and was dredged in 1961 to allow larger cargo vessels to dock. The first bridge, Al Maktoum, opened two years later.

Four bridges, a tunnel and both Dubai metro lines connect the two banks, but by far the most atmospheric way to get across (especially at or after sunset) is the Dh1 ride aboard a motorised abra. These traditional wooden boats shuttle between the Deira and Bur Dubai souqs in a quick five minutes.

Sights

Spice Souq   MARKET

1 ◉ MAP P36, B2

Steps from the Deira Old Souk abra station, the sound of Arabic chatter bounces around the lanes of this small covered market as vendors work hard to unload cardamom, saffron and other aromatic herbs photogenically stored in burlap sacks alongside dried fruit, nuts, incense burners, henna kits and *sheesha*. Away from the tourist-oriented main thoroughfare, the tiny shops also sell groceries, plastics and other household goods to locals and sailors from the dhows. (btwn Baniyas Rd, Al Ras Rd & Al Abra St; ⊙roughly 9am-10pm Sat-Thu, 4-10pm Fri; Ⓜ Al Ras)

Dhow Wharfage   HARBOUR

2 ◉ MAP P36, B2

Stroll down the Creek for photogenic close-ups of dozens of brightly coloured dhows docked next to the Deira souqs to load and unload everything from air-conditioners and chewing gum to car tyres. This type of long flat wooden cargo boat has done trade across the Gulf and Indian Ocean for centuries, trading with such countries as Iran, Iraq, India, Somalia and Oman. (along Baniyas Rd; Ⓜ Al Ras)

Perfume Souq   MARKET

3 ◉ MAP P36, C2

Several blocks with a preponderance of perfume shops hardly warrants the title 'souq', yet these stores sell a staggering range of Arabic *attars,* oil-based perfumes that are usually kept in large bulbous bottles and siphoned off into elegant flacons upon purchase. The most precious scents contain *oud,* from a resinous hardwood called agarwood, formed by the Southeast Asian aquilaria tree. (Naif Rd & Al Soor St; ⏱10am-1pm & 3-10pm; Ⓜ Palm Deira)

Women's Museum
MUSEUM

4 ◉ MAP P36, C2

Try on a *burka* (long, enveloping garment), find out about Ousha bint Khalifa Al Suwaidi (the UAE's most celebrated female poet) and learn about the achievements of local women in the fields of science, trade, education, politics and literature at the region's first museum to train the spotlight on women. The museum is tucked

into the warren of lanes north of the Gold Souq and a bit hard to find. Look for signs in the souq or on Al Khaleej Rd. (Bait Al Banat; 📞04 234 2342; www.womenmuseumuae.com; Sikka 9 & 28; Dhs20; ⏱10am-7pm Sat-Thu)

Museum of the Poet Al Oqaili
MUSEUM

5 ◉ MAP P36, B2

In 1923 this beautifully restored home tucked into the narrow lanes on the edge of the Spice Souq (p35) became the home of Saudi-born Mubarak bin Al Oqaili (1875–1954), one of the most important classical Arabic poets. A bilingual exhibit charts milestones in his life and work and also displays original manuscripts

Abra (wooden ferries)

and personal belongings such as his desk, a gun and a pen. (📞04 515 5000; www.dubaiculture.gov.ae/en; Sikka 21b, Spice Souq; admission free; ⏱8am-2pm Sun-Thu; Ⓜ Al Ras)

Naif Market
MARKET

6 ◉ MAP P36, C2

Although the historic Naif Souq burned down in 2008 and was replaced by this mall-style version, it's still an atmospheric place to shop and is especially popular with local women looking for bargain-priced *abeyyas* (full-length robes) and accessories such as hair extensions, costume jewellery and henna products. (btwn Naif South, 9a & Deira Sts; ⏱8.30am-11.30pm; Ⓜ Baniyas Square)

Covered Souq
MARKET

7 ◉ MAP P36, C2

Despite the name, this souq is not really covered at all; rather it's an amorphous warren of narrow lanes criss-crossing a few square blocks roughly bounded by Naif Rd, Al Soor St, 18th St and Al Sabkha Rd. Even if you're not keen on cheap textiles, faux Gucci, *kandouras* (long traditional robes), plastic toys and cheap trainers, you'll likely be entertained by the high-energy street scene. (south of Naif Rd; ⏱9am-10pm; Ⓜ Palm Deira)

Al Mamzar Beach Park
BEACH

8 ◉ MAP P36, F2

This lushly landscaped beach park consists of a string of five lovely sandy sweeps and comes with plenty of infrastructure, including a swimming pool, playgrounds, picnic areas with barbecues, water sports and bicycle rentals, snack bars, lawns, Smart Palms for wi-fi access and air-conditioned cabanas (Dhs150 to Dhs200 per day, on Beach 4). (📞04 296 6201; Al Mamzar Creek, Deira; per person/car Dhs5/30, pool adult/child Dhs10/5; ⏱8am-10pm Sun-Wed, to 11pm Thu-Sat; Ⓟ)

Heritage House
MUSEUM

9 ◉ MAP P36, B1

Closed for renovation at the time of writing, this 1890 courtyard house once belonged to Sheikh Ahmed bin Dalmouk, a wealthy pearl merchant and founder of the adjacent Al Ahmadiya School, Dubai's oldest learning pen. Built from coral and gypsum, it wraps around a central courtyard flanked by verandahs to keep direct sunlight out, and sports lofty wind towers for cooling the air. If workers are on site, ask nicely and you may be able to take a peek inside. (📞04 226 0286; www.dubaiculture.gov.ae/en; Al Ahmadiya St; Ⓜ Al Ras)

National Bank of Dubai
ARCHITECTURE

10 ◉ MAP P36, C4

In 2007 the National Bank of Dubai merged with Emirates Bank to form Emirates NBD, but its headquarters remains in this shimmering landmark overlooking the Creek. Designed by Carlos Ott and

Getting Off the Main Grid

Easily reached by metro, Al Muteena St is one of the most enticing walking streets in town, with wide pavements, palm trees and a park-like strip running along its centre. In the Iraqi restaurants and cafes you'll see *masgouf* – a whole fish sliced in half, seasoned and barbecued over an open flame. The *sheesha* cafes have to be seen to be believed: some feature rock gardens, dangling fronds and artificial lakes. Nearby Al Muraqqabat Rd brims with superb Syrian, Lebanese and Palestinian eateries. A bit south of here, Al Rigga Rd is also packed with promising eateries and also boasts a lively street scene.

completed in 1997, it combines simple shapes to represent a dhow with a billowing sail, while the real-life dhows plying the Creek are reflected in its gold-coated glass facade. Best at sunset. (Emirates NBD; Baniyas Rd; **M** Union)

Al Ahmadiya School   MUSEUM

11 ◉ MAP P36, B1

Closed indefinitely for renovation, Dubai's first public primary school was founded by the pearl merchant Sheikh Ahmed bin Dalmouk and welcomed its first pupils (all boys) in 1912. Decades later Dubai's current ruler, Sheikh Mohammed, was among those who squeezed behind the wooden desks. The building itself is lovely with intricately carved courtyard arches, heavy ornamented doors and decorative gypsum panels. It remained in use as a school until the student body outgrew the premises in 1963.

No reopening date had been announced at the time of writing. (Al Ahmadiya St; **M** Al Ras)

Eating

Aroos Damascus   SYRIAN $

12 ✕ MAP P36, D4

A Dubai restaurant serving Syrian food to adoring crowds since 1980 must be doing something right. A perfect meal would start with hummus and a *fattoosh* salad before moving on to a plate of succulent grilled kebabs. Huge outdoor patio; cool flickering neon; busy until the wee hours. (☎04 221 9825; cnr Al Muraqqabat & Al Jazeira Rd; sandwiches Dhs4-20, mezze Dhs14-35, mains Dhs15-50; ⏰7am-3am; **M** Salah Al Din)

Aseelah   EMIRATI $$

13 ✕ MAP P36, C4

With its mix of traditional and modern Emirati cuisine, this stylish restaurant ticks all the right boxes. Many dishes feature a local spice mix called *bezar,* including the date-stuffed chicken leg and the camel stew. To go the whole, well, goat, order *ouzi,* an entire animal filled with legumes and nuts, slow-cooked for 24 hours. Nice terrace. (📞04 205 7033; www.radissonblu.com; Baniyas Rd, 2nd fl, Radisson Blu Hotel, Al Rigga; mains Dhs45-195; ⏱12.30-4pm & 6.30-11.15pm; 🅿🛜; Ⓜ Union, Baniyas Square)

Al Tawasol YEMENI $

14 ❌ MAP P36, D6

Camp out on the carpet in the main dining room or in a private 'Bedouin-style tent' at this traditional Yemeni eatery. Staff will spread a flimsy plastic sheet to protect the rug from earthy dishes such as turmeric-laced rice topped with curried mutton or oven-roasted chicken *mandi* (rice topped with spicy stew). Ask for a spoon if eating with your hands doesn't appeal. (📞04 295 9797; Abu Bakar al Siddiq Rd, Al Rigga; mains Dhs25-75; ⏱11am-1am; Ⓜ Al Rigga)

Qwaider Al Nabulsi ARABIC $

15 ❌ MAP P36, D5

Behind the garish neon facade, this place at first looks like a sweet shop (the *kunafa*, a vermicelli-like pastry soaked in syrup, is great), but it also has a full menu of Arabic delicacies like scrumptious *musakhan* (chicken pie) and sesame-seed-coated falafel *mahshi* (stuffed with chilli paste). The latter's fluffy filling is coloured green from the addition of parsley and other herbs. (📞04 227 7760; Al Muraqqabat St; snacks Dhs10-17, mains Dhs28-50; ⏱8am-2am; 👬; Ⓜ Al Rigga, Salah Al Din)

Xiao Wei Yang Hotpot CHINESE $$

16 ❌ MAP P36, C3

Next to Twin Towers, this authentic hotpot restaurant works like this: a bubbling broth inspired by Genghis Khan is placed on a hot plate on your table. Create a dipping sauce from a mix of satay, garlic, coriander, chilli and spices. Choose ingredients (fish balls, crab, tofu, lotus root, beef slices) to cook in the cauldron. Dip and enjoy! (Little Lamb Mongolian Hotpot; 📞04 221 5111; www.facebook.com/pg/xiaoweiyangdubai; Baniyas Rd; hotpots Dhs28-32, meats Dhs36-48, combos Dhs98-148; ⏱11am-1am; Ⓜ Baniyas Square)

Thai Kitchen THAI $$

17 ❌ MAP P36, C8

The decor is decidedly un-Thai, with black-lacquer tables, a swooping wave-form ceiling and not a branch of bamboo. Led by Supattra Boonsrang for more than a decade, the cooks here know their stuff: dishes are inspired by Bangkok street eats and served in sizes that are perfect for grazing and sharing. The Friday brunch is tops too. (📞04 602 1234; www.dubai.park.hyatt.com; Dubai Creek Club St, Park Hyatt Dubai; small plates Dhs42-70, Fri brunch Dhs255-395; ⏱noon-11.45pm; 🅿🛜🍴; Ⓜ Deira City Centre)

Al Mansour Dhow
INTERNATIONAL $$$

18 🍴 MAP P36, C3

Take in the skyline on this moving feast aboard a trad wooden dhow decorated with bands of twinkling lights. Soulful Arabic song accompanies the lavish buffet spread that's heavy on Arabic and Indian choices. There's a full bar and an upper-deck *sheesha* lounge for chilling. Board outside the **Radisson Blu Hotel** (www.radissonblu.com; Baniyas Rd; MUnion, Baniyas Square), which operates this dinner cruise. (📞04 205 7033; 2hr dinner cruise adult/child Dhs185/100; 🕗8pm; P🛜)

Sumibiya
KOREAN $$$

19 🍴 MAP P36, C3

At Dubai's first *yakiniku*-style restaurant is interactive foodie fun for families and groups. Every stone table has a recessed gas grill where you cook your own meat, then pair it with sauces and condiments. The set menus featuring beef, chicken, fish or lamb, along with salad, rice, soup, kimchi and dessert, are good value. (📞04 205 7033; www.radissonblu.com; Baniyas Rd, Radisson Blu Hotel; set menus Dhs125; 🕗7-11pm Wed-Sat; P🛜; MUnion, Baniyas Square)

Shabestan
IRANIAN $$$

20 🍴 MAP P36, C4

This long-standing traditional Persian lair has a lovely panorama of

Deira Eating

Middle Eastern sharing-style meal

glittering lights unfolding over the Creek. Take your sweet time as you tuck into classics such as *fesenjan* (chicken in walnut-pomegranate sauce) or *ghormeh sabzi* (lamb stew) and finish up with a scoop of saffron ice cream. (📞04 222 7171; www.radissonblu.com; Baniyas Rd, Radisson Blu Hotel; mains Dhs105-185; ⏱12.15-3.15pm & 7.30-11.30pm; 🅿🛜; Ⓜ Union, Baniyas Square)

Sadaf Iranian Sweets
DESSERTS $

21 ❌ MAP P36, D5

Tucked into a small arcade, this little shop brims with spices, nuts, saffron, teas and other goodies from Iran, but insiders flock here for *faloodeh,* a mouthwatering dessert consisting of crunchy vermicelli-sized noodles drenched in a syrup made from rosewater, lemon and sugar and served with a scoop of saffron ice cream. (📞04 229 7000; Rigga Al Buteen Plaza, Al Maktoum Rd; ⏱8am-midnight; Ⓜ Al Rigga)

Afghan Khorasan Kabab
AFGHANI $

22 ❌ MAP P36, C2

Big hunks of meat – mutton or chicken – charred on foot-long skewers are paired with Afghan *pulao* (rice pilaf), chewy bread and sauces. That's it. For added authenticity, eat with your hands and sit upstairs in the carpeted *majlis* (reception room). It's located in an alley behind Al Ghurair Mosque.

(📞04 359 0003; off Deira St; mains Dhs19-40; ⏱11.30am-1am; Ⓜ Baniyas Square)

Ashiana
INDIAN $$$

23 ❌ MAP P36, C4

This oldie but goodie serves modernised Indian fare in an elegant, dimly lit dining room that radiates the intimacy of an old private villa. The menu spans the arc from richly nuanced curries and succulent kebabs to fluffy biryanis and inspired shareable mains such as *raan lucknowi* (slow-cooked, 48-hour marinated lamb), all beautifully presented. (📞04 207 1733; www.ashianadubai.com; Baniyas Rd, ground fl, Sheraton Dubai Creek Hotel & Towers; mains Dhs58-148; ⏱noon-3pm & 7-11pm; 🛜🍴; Ⓜ Union)

Drinking

Irish Village
IRISH PUB

24 🅟 MAP P36, C8

This always-buzzing pub, with its Irish-main-street facade made with materials imported straight from the Emerald Isle, has been a Dubai institution since 1996. There's Guinness and Kilkenny on tap, lovely gardens around a petite lake, the occasional live band and plenty of pub grub to keep your tummy in a state of contentment. (📞04 282 4750; www.theirishvillage. com; 31A St, Garhoud; ⏱11am-1am Sat-Wed, to 2am Thu & Fri; 🛜; Ⓜ GGICO)

Bartender at Terrace (p46)

QDs

BAR

25 MAP P36, C8

Watch the ballet of lighted dhows floating by while sipping cocktails at this always-fun outdoor Creek-side lounge deck where carpets and cushions set an inviting mood. In summer, keep cool in an air-conditioned tent. Great for sheesha-holics too. (04 295 6000; www.dubaigolf.com; Dubai Creek Club St, Dubai Creek Golf & Yacht Club, Garhoud; sheesha Dhs65; ⌚5pm-2am Sun-Wed, to 3am Thu & Sat, 1pm-3am Fri; ; Deira City Centre)

Cielo Sky Lounge

BAR

26 MAP P36, C8

Looking very much like a futuristic James Bond–worthy yacht, Cielo flaunts a sultry, romantic vibe

helped by the bobbing yachts below and the cool views of the Dubai skyline across the Creek. One of the chicest spots on this side of town to ring in the night with sundowners and global bar bites. (04 416 1800; www.cielodubai.com; Dubai Creek Club St, Dubai Creek Golf & Yacht Club; ⌚4pm-2am Sep-May; ; Deira City Centre)

Juice World

JUICE BAR

27 MAP P36, D5

Need some A.S.S., Man Kiwi or Viagra? Then head down to this actually very wholesome Saudi juice bar famous not only for its 150 fantastically creative liquid potions but also for its outrageous fruit sculptures. There's an entire room of them: must be seen to be believed. The big outdoor terrace offers primo people-watching. (📞04 299 9465; www.juiceworld.ae; Al Rigga St; ⏰1pm-2am Sat-Wed, to 3am Thu & Fri; 🅼Al Rigga)

Terrace
BAR

28 🚇 MAP P36, C8

With its sleek design, floor-to-ceiling windows and canopy-covered deck, the Terrace itself provides plenty of design eye candy before you've even taken in the chic crowd or the dreamy sunset views across the Creek. (📞04 602 1814; http://dubai.park.hyatt.com; Dubai Creek Club St, Park Hyatt Dubai; ⏰6pm-2am; 🛜; 🅼Deira City Centre)

Issimo
SPORTS BAR

29 🚇 MAP P36, C5

Illuminated blue flooring, black-leather sofas and sleek chrome finishing lend an edgy look to this sports-and-martini bar. If you're not into sports – or TV – you may find the giant screens distracting. (📞04 227 1111; Baniyas Rd, Hilton Dubai Creek; ⏰3pm-1am; 🛜; 🅼Al Rigga, Union)

Shopping

Deira City Centre
MALL

30 🅰 MAP P36, C7

Though other malls are bigger and flashier, Deira City Centre remains a stalwart for its logical layout and wide selection of shops, from big-name chains like H&M and Zara to locally owned stores carrying quality carpets, souvenirs

and handicrafts. (📞04 295 1010; www.deiracitycentre.com; Baniyas Rd; ⏰10am-10pm Sun-Wed, to midnight Thu-Sat; 🛜; 🅼Deira City Centre)

Al Ghurair Centre
MALL

31 🅰 MAP P36, D4

Dubai's oldest shopping mall opened in 1980 and is a lot less flashy than its newer cousins despite an expansion that doubled its number of shops to 300. Aside from the expected Western labels, these include speciality stores selling national dress and Arabic fragrances. There's also a food court with 70 outlets and an eight-screen multiplex. (📞800 24227; www.alghuraircentre.com; cnr Al Rigga & Omar bin al Khattab Rds; ⏰10am-10pm Sun-Wed, to midnight Thu-Sat; 🅼Union, Salah Al Din, Al Rigga)

Mikyajy
COSMETICS

32 🅰 MAP P36, D8

You feel like you're walking into a chocolate gift-box at tiny Mikyajy, the region's home-grown make-up brand. Although calibrated to Middle Eastern tastes and complexions, the vivid colours will brighten up any face. (📞04 295 7844; www.mikyajy.com; Baniyas Rd, 2nd fl, Deira City Centre; ⏰10am-10pm Sun-Wed, to midnight Thu-Sat; 🛜; 🅼Deira City Centre)

Damas
JEWELLERY

33 🅰 MAP P36, D8

Damas may not be the most innovative jeweller in Dubai, but

A Primer on Bargaining

o Compare prices at a few shops or stalls so you get an idea of what things cost and how much you're willing to pay.

o When you're interested in buying an item, don't show too much enthusiasm or you'll never get the price down.

o Don't pay the first price quoted. This is actually considered arrogant.

o Start below the price you wish to pay so you have room to compromise – but don't quote too low or the vendor may feel insulted. A good rule of thumb is to cut the first suggested price in half and go from there. Expect to finish up with a discount of 20% to 30%.

o If you intend to buy more than one item, use this as a bargaining chip – the more you buy, the better the discount.

o Take your time and stay relaxed. You can come away with an enjoyable experience whether you end up with a bargain or not.

o If negotiations aren't going to plan, simply smile and say goodbye – often the vendor will follow and suggest a compromise price.

with more than 50 shops, it's essentially omnipresent. Among the diamonds and gold, look for elaborate bridal jewellery as well as classic pieces and big-designer names such as Fabergé and Tiffany. (📞04 295 3848; Baniyas Rd, Deira City Centre; ⏰10am-10pm Sun-Wed, to midnight Thu-Sat, 🍴, Ⓜ Deira City Centre)

Gift Village DEPARTMENT STORE

34 🔒 MAP P36, C3

If you've spent all your money on Jimmy Choo shoes and bling at the Gold Souq and need a new inflight bag, this cut-price place has a great range. It also stocks cosmetics, shoes, clothing, toys, sports goods, jewellery and ami-

ably kitsch souvenirs, all imported from China, Thailand and Turkey. (📞04 294 6858; www.gift-village. com; 14th St, Baniyas Sq; ⏰9am-1am Sun-Thu, 9am-noon & 2pm-2am Fri, Ⓜ Baniyas Square)

Women's Secret CLOTHING

35 🔒 MAP P36, C8

This sassy Spanish label is popular for its global-pop-art-inspired underwear, swimwear and nightwear. Expect anything from cute Mexican cross-stitched bra-and-pants sets to Moroccan-style kaftanlike nightdresses. (📞04 295 9665; Baniyas Rd, 1st fl, Deira City Centre; ⏰10am-10pm Sun-Wed, to midnight Thu-Sat; Ⓜ Deira City Centre)

Explore
Bur Dubai

Historic Bur Dubai provides an eye-opening journey into the city's past, with its most intriguing areas flanking the waterfront. Delve into the city's past in the Al Fahidi and Shindagha historic areas and Dubai Museum, then watch the abras (traditional wooden ferries) depart for quick cross-Creek rides to the Deira souqs. The streets of the surrounding Meena Bazaar district are nirvana for adventurous foodies and also harbour a bustling souq specialising in textiles. For a special treat, book ahead for a meal hosted by the Sheikh Mohammed Centre for Cultural Understanding to meet locals and eat home-cooked Emirati food.

Away from the Creek, Bur Dubai becomes rather non-descript, if not without its highlights. Near upmarket BurJuman Centre mall, densely populated Karama offers great bargain shopping and more bustling eateries serving princely meals at pauper prices. It segues into Zabeel Park, one of the city's largest patches of green and home to the new Dubai Frame observation tower. The most eye-catching structures further east are the Egyptian-themed Wafi Mall and the pyramid-shaped Raffles hotel.

Getting There & Around
Dubai Metro's Red and Green Lines intersect at BurJuman, with the latter continuing into historic Bur Dubai before crossing the Creek to Deira. Abras link Bur Dubai to Deira.

Ⓜ Al Fahidi/Al Ghubaiba

🚤 Two stations near the Bur Dubai Souq

Bur Dubai Map on p56

Abra (wooden ferry) crossing Dubai Creek TASFOTONL/SHUTTERSTOCK ©

Top Sight
Dubai Museum

This museum is your ticket to learning about Dubai's turbo-evolution from fishing and pearling village to global centre of commerce, finance and tourism. It's housed in the Al Fahidi Fort, built around 1800 and considered the oldest surviving structure in town. A walk-through mock souq, exhibits on Bedouin life, and a room highlighting the importance of the sea illustrate the pre-oil era.

◉ MAP P56, E2

☑ 04 353 1862

Al Fahidi St

adult/child Dhs3/1

🕐 8.30am-8.30pm Sat-Thu, 2.30-8.30pm Fri

Ⓜ Al Fahidi

Al Fahidi Fort

Built from coral and limestone and fortified by three towers, the crenellated citadel had not only defensive purposes but also served as the residence of the local rulers until 1896. It was then turned into an arsenal for the fledging city's artillery and weapons and also went through a stint as a prison. The fort is depicted on the 100-dirham note.

Courtyard

The fort is entered via a sturdy teak door festooned with brass spikes that leads to the central courtyard dotted with bronze cannons, traditional wooden fishing boats and traditional dwellings. Other doors lead to modest displays of instruments and handcrafted weapons.

Souq Dioramas

In the actual museum, you cross the deck of a dhow to enter a mock souq with life-size dioramas depicting shopkeepers and craftspeople at work, enhanced by light and sound effects, historical photos and grainy documentary footage.

Pearl-Diving Exhibit

Learn how pearl divers wore merely nose clips and leather gloves while descending to extraordinary depths in this fascinating display that incorporates historical footage of divers at work.

Archaeological Finds

The final section showcases finds from ancient settlements at Jumeirah, Al Qusais and other local archaeological sites. Most are believed to have been established here between 2000 and 1000 BC.

★ Top Tips

o Visit early in the morning or late in the afternoon to avoid tour groups.

o Check out the courtyard walls, made with traditional coral and gypsum.

o Don't bother with a tour guide: exhibits are sufficiently well explained in English.

o Take the kids! They'll love the sound effects, films and detailed dioramas.

o Skip the gift shop and head for the nearby souq instead.

✕ Take a Break

For a tasty breakfast or light meal, head to the courtyard of the charismatic Arabian Tea House (p55). The best butter chicken is served at Sind Punjab (p62), the oldest family eatery in the Indian-dominated Meena Bazaar quarter.

Top Experience 📖✎
Al Fahidi Historic District

Traffic fades to a quiet hum in the labyrinthine lanes of this restored heritage arear. The sand-coloured houses lining the lanes are topped with wind towers, which provide natural air-conditioning. Today, there are about 50 buildings containing crafts shops, cultural exhibits, courtyard cafes, art galleries and two boutique hotels. Above it all rises the distinctive ornate flat dome and slender minaret of the alabaster-white Diwan Mosque.

◎ MAP P56, F2

Al Fahidi St

admission free

Ⓜ Al Fahidi

Alserkal Cultural Foundation

At this dynamic **cultural space** (☎04 353 5922; www.alserkalculturalfoundation.com; Heritage House No 13; admission free; ☺9am-7pm) galleries showcase traditional and cutting-edge works by local and international artists in rooms orbiting a central courtyard with an arty cafe. Most of the art is for sale and there's also a small shop stocking gifts.

Coffee Museum

This cute private **museum** (☎04 353 8777; www.coffeemuseum.ae; admission free; ☺9am-5pm Sat-Thu) in a historic Emirati home offers an aromatic bean-based journey around the world and back in time. You can even sample freshly brewed Ethiopian coffee prepared by staff in traditional garb (Dhs10).

Majlis Gallery

Dubai's oldest **fine art gallery** (☎04 353 6233; www.themajlisgallery.com; Al Fahidi St; admission free; ☺10am-6pm Sat-Thu) presents mainly paintings and sculpture by international artists inspired by the region, as well as high-quality pottery, glass and other crafts. It was founded in 1989 by British expat Allison Collins who first came to Dubai in 1976. Renowned Emirati artist Abdul Qader Al Rais had one of his first exhibits here.

Coin Museum

This petite **museum** (☎04 392 0093; www.dubaiculture.gov.ae/en; admission free; ☺8am-2pm Sun-Thu) presents nearly 500 rare coins from throughout the Middle East, including Egypt, Turkey and Morocco. The oldest were minted during the Arab-Sasanian era in the 7th century.

★ **Top Tips**

o Don't be shy about pushing open some of those heavy doors and finding out what's behind them.

o Shutterbugs should visit early in the morning or late in the afternoon for the best light conditions.

o Look for a short section of the old city wall from 1800, which looks a bit like a dinosaur tail.

o Admission to all museums and exhibits is free.

✗ **Take a Break**

Have a mint lemonade or snack at the cafe in the charming courtyard cafe of the Alserkal Cultural Foundation or relax in the sun-dappled garden of the Arabian Tea House (62).

Walking Tour 🚶

Bur Dubai Waterside Walk

This heritage walk of Dubai's oldest area kicks off in the Al Fahidi Historic District, where you can wander around the atmospheric narrow lanes and peek into the renovated wind-tower houses. From here the route ticks off several of Dubai's most interesting traditional sights along the Creek and provides a glimpse into the pre-oil era with nary a shopping mall, skyscraper or ski slope in sight.

Walk Facts

Start Al Fahidi Historic District

End Barjeel Heritage Guest House

Length 3km; two to three hours

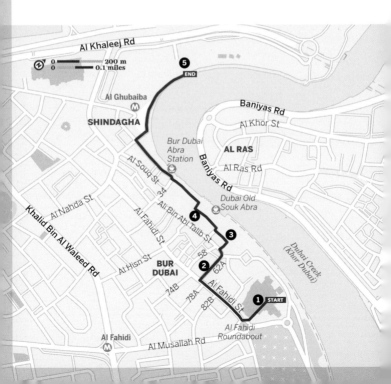

❶ Al Fahidi Historic District

Kick off your tour with a leisurely wander along the narrow lanes of one of Dubai's oldest neighbourhoods and check out the traditional wind-tower architecture. Pop into small museums like the **Coffee Museum** (p53) or galleries like **XVA Gallery** (p60) and the **Al-serkal Cultural Foundation** (p53) before stopping for refreshments in the enchanting walled garden of the **Arabian Tea House** (p62).

❷ Dubai Museum

Wrap up the historic district by checking out the **Majlis Gallery** (p55), the oldest art space in Dubai, before continuing west along Al Fahidi St to the **Dubai Museum** (p50), which introduces the history, heritage and development of this burgeoning city. Turn left as you exit the museum and peer towards Dubai's tallest minaret, atop the **Grand Mosque**.

❸ Hindi Lane

Follow the lane to the mosque's right-hand side before ducking into teensy **Hindi Lane** (p60), a vibrant and colourful alley lined with pint-sized shops selling religious paraphernalia. This alley is home to Dubai's only Hindu temple.

❹ Bur Dubai Souq

Exiting Hindi Lane takes you to the wooden arcades of the **Bur Dubai Souq** (p60) and its colourful textile and trinket shops. Lug your loot to the waterfront and snap pictures of the abras at the Dubai Old Souk abra station before following the Creek north to the Shindagha Historic District.

❺ Shindagha Historic District

Lined with the historic former residences of Dubai's ruling family, this waterfront area is undergoing extensive redevelopment. Ignore the dust and make your way to the splendid **Sheikh Saeed Al Maktoum House** (p58) to marvel at the amazing photo collection of old Dubai, then check out the beautifully displayed finds from Dubai's latest desert dig at the new **Saruq Al Hadid Archaeology Museum** (p58). Wrap up with a snack or a juice at the **Barjeel Heritage Guest House** while watching the timeless ballet of boat traffic from your terrace table.

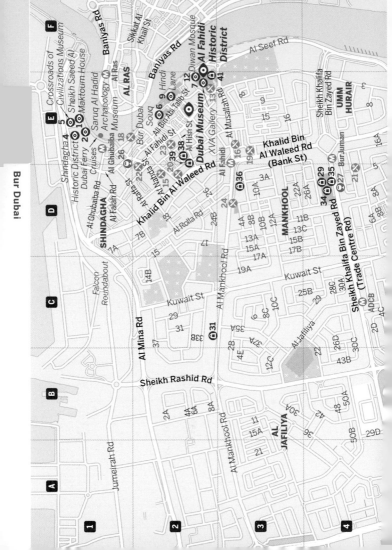

Bur Dubai

Jumeirah Rd

Al Mina Rd

Baniyas Rd

Falcon Roundabout

Crossroads of Civilizations Museum
Sheikh Saeed Al Maktoum House
Saruq Al Hadid Archaeology Museum
Al Ghubaiba Museum

Shindagha 4
Historic District Dubai Ferry Cruises

SHINDAGHA

Al Ghubaiba Rd
Al Falah Rd
Al Rafa St · Al Nahda St

Baniyas Rd
Sikkat Al Khail St

AL RAS
Al Ras

Bur Dubai Souq

Al Bin Abi Talib St
Al Fahidi St
Al Hisn St

Al Fahidi Historic District

Diwan Mosque
Hindi Lane

Dubai Museum

XVA Gallery 13
Al Musallah Rd

Al Seef Rd

Sheikh Khalifa Bin Zayed Rd

UMM HURAIR

Khalid Bin Al Waleed Rd (Bank St)

Al Fahidi

Bur Juman

MANKHOOL

Khalid Bin Al Waleed Rd

Al Rolla Rd

Al Mankhool Rd

Kuwait St

Kuwait St

Al Jafiliya

Sheikh Rashid Rd

AL JAFILIYA

Al Mankhool Rd

Sheikh Khalifa Bin Zayed Rd (Trade Centre Rd)

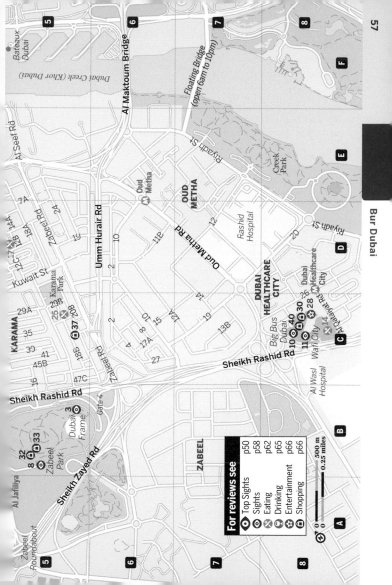

Bur Dubai

Bateaux Dubai

Dubai Creek (Khor Dubai)

Al Maktoum Bridge

Floating Bridge
(open 6am to 10pm)

Al Seef Rd

Riyadh St

Creek Park

F

E

Oud Metha

OUD METHA

Rashid Hospital

DUBAI HEALTHCARE CITY

Dubai Healthcare City

Riyadh St

Big Bus Dubai

Wafi City

Al Qataiyat Rd

Al Wasl Hospital

Umm Hurair Rd

Oud Metha Rd

Zabeel Rd

Kuwait St

Karama Park

KARAMA

Sheikh Rashid Rd

Sheikh Rashid Rd

Zabeel Park

Dubai Frame

Al Jaffiliya

Gate 4

Zabeel Rd

ZABEEL

Sheikh Zayed Rd

Zabeel Roundabout

7A

14A

12B

18A

2A

12C 12B 17A

29A

35

39

41

45B

16

47C

18S

20B

23B

26

37

10

2

1F

2

19

14

21

15

19

13B

27

4

8

17A

10

12

20

26

28

14

30

40

11

32

8

33

3

For reviews see

◉	Top Sights	p50
◎	Sights	p58
⊗	Eating	p62
✕	Drinking	p65
✦	Entertainment	p66
⊞	Shopping	p66

500 m
0.25 miles

A   B   C   D   E   F

5   6   7   8

Sights

Sheikh Saeed Al Maktoum House

MUSEUM

1 MAP P56, E1

This grand courtyard house served as the residence of Sheikh Saeed, the grandfather of current Dubai ruler Sheikh Mohammed bin Rashid, from 1912 until his death in 1958. Today, the architectural marvel houses an excellent collection of pre-oil boom photographs of Dubai taken in the souqs, on the Creek and at traditional celebrations. There are also some insightful private images of the ruling Al Maktoum clan. Other rooms feature coins, stamps and documents dating back as far as 1791. (📞04 393 7139; Shindagha Waterfront, Shindagha Historic District; adult/child Dhs3/1; ☺8am-8.30pm Sat-Thu, 3-9.30pm Fri; Ⓜ Al Ghubaiba)

Saruq Al Hadid Archaeology Museum

MUSEUM

2 MAP P56, E1

Only discovered in 2002, Saruq Al Hadid sits deep in the desert sands of the southern reaches of the Dubai emirate and is believed to have been an iron-age metal 'factory' in operation between 1300 and 800 BC. Excavations have thus far yielded mostly swords, axe heads, daggers and other weapons, some of which are on display in this modern museum. Videos documenting the site's discovery and featuring interviews with archaeologists about their latest findings and theories provide further depth. (📞ext 203 04 359 5612; www.saruqalhadid.ae; Shindagha Waterfront; adult/child Dhs20/10; ☺8am-8pm Sun-Wed, to 2pm Thu & Sat; Ⓜ Al Ghubaiba)

Emirati Culture Demystified

Open doors, open minds: such is the motto of the **Sheikh Mohammed Centre for Cultural Understanding** (📞04 353 6666; www. cultures.ae; House 26, Al Musalla Rd; heritage/Creekside tours Dhs80/275, meals Dhs90-120; ☺9am-5pm Sun-Thu, to 1pm Sat; Ⓜ Al Fahidi), an institution founded by Dubai's ruler Sheikh Mohammed bin Rashid in 1998 to help visitors understand the traditions and customs of the United Arab Emirates. It conducts guided tours of the Al Fahidi Historic District and Jumeirah Mosque and also hosts hugely popular cultural breakfasts and lunches where you also get a chance to meet, ask questions of, and exchange ideas with Emiratis. Reservations essential.

Zabeel Park (p60)

Dubai Frame

VIEWPOINT

3 ◉ MAP P56, B5

Opened on 1 January 2018, this 150m rectangular 'picture frame' sits in Zabeel Park (p60), right between historic and modern Dubai, and provides grand views of both parts of the city. Galleries on the ground floor tell the story of Dubai (the past) before visitors are whisked up to a viewing platform at roof level (the present). The final stop is another gallery depicting a vision of Dubai 50 years from now (the future). (www.thedubaiframe. com; Gate 3, Zabeel Park; adult/child Dhs50/20; ⏲9am-9pm; Ⓜ Al Jafiliya)

Shindagha Historic District

AREA

4 ◉ MAP P56, E1

Strategically located at the mouth of Dubai Creek, Shindagha was where the ruling sheikhs and the city elite lived until the 1950s. While some homes have been reconstructed and recast as museums, most of the area is fenced off until at least 2018 while it is being turned into a heritage district. Once the dust has settled, there will be a new Shindagha Museum as well as additional exhibits, heritage hotels and restaurants. (Shindagha Waterfront; Ⓜ Al Ghubaiba)

Crossroads of Civilizations Museum MUSEUM

5 ⊙ MAP P56, E1

This private museum in the Shindagha Historic District (p59) illustrates Dubai's historic role as a trading link between East and West. On display are hundreds of artefacts from the Ubaids, Greeks, Romans, Babylonians and other civilisations that passed through the region. (☎04 393 4440; www.themuseum.ae; Al Khaleej Rd; Dhs30; ⏰9am-5pm Sat-Thu; Ⓜ Al Ghubaiba)

Bur Dubai Souq SOUQ

6 ⊙ MAP P56, E2

Dubai's oldest souq flanks a central arcade canopied by an ornately carved wooden roof. Friday evenings here are especially lively, as it turns into a virtual crawling carnival with expat workers loading up on socks, pashminas, T-shirts and knock-off Calvins on their day off. In a section known as the **Textile Souq** you can stock up on fabrics – silk, cotton, satin, velvet – at very reasonable prices. (btwn Bur Dubai waterfront & Ali bin Abi Talib St; ⏰8am-1pm & 4-10pm Sat-Thu, 4-10pm Fri; Ⓜ Al Ghubaiba)

XVA Gallery GALLERY

7 ⊙ MAP P56, E2

Tucked into the Al Fahidi Historic District (p52) since 2003, XVA has a knack for ferreting out top-notch up-and-comers from around the Middle East and India. Works often express the artists' cultural identities and challenge viewers' preconceptions. It also participates in prestigious art fairs such as Art Basel and Art London. (☎04 353 5383; www.xvagallery.com; XVA Guesthouse, Al Fahidi Historic District, off Al Fahidi St; ⏰10am-6pm; Ⓜ Al Fahidi)

Zabeel Park PARK

8 ⊙ MAP P56, B5

This sprawling park, where lots of palms and other greenery provide plenty of shade, is a weekend family favourite. It brims with activity zones, including a pretty lake with boat rides, an adventure playground, covered barbecue areas, a jogging track and a miniature train. (☎04 398 6888; Gate 1, off Sheikh Khalifa bin Zayed Rd; Dhs5; ⏰8am-11pm Sat-Wed, to 11.30pm Thu-Fri; 🚻; Ⓜ Al Jafiliya)

Hindi Lane STREET

9 ⊙ MAP P56, E2

Until the completion of a new temple in Abu Dhabi, only a tiny and ageing double-shrine, tucked behind the Grand Mosque since 1958, serves the UAE's nearly 3 million Hindus. Dedicated to Shiva and Krishna, it is entered via a narrow and colourful alleyway colloquially known as Hindi Lane and lined with vendors selling religious paraphernalia and offerings, including baskets of fruit, flower garlands, gold-embossed holy images, sacred ash and sandalwood paste. (off Ali bin Abi Talib St; Ⓜ Al Fahidi, Al Ghubaiba)

The History of Al Fahidi

Previously known as Bastakia Quarter, the Al Fahidi Historic District was built in the early 1900s by merchants from the Persian town of Bastak, who settled in Dubai to take advantage of tax breaks granted by the sheikh. By the 1970s, though, the buildings had fallen into disrepair and residents began moving on to newer, more comfortable neighbourhoods. Dedicated locals, expats and even Prince Charles prevented the area's demolition in the 1980s. To learn more, sign up for a guided tour with the **Sheikh Mohammed Centre for Cultural Understanding** (p58).

Big Bus Dubai
BUS

10 ⊙ MAP P56, C8

These hop-on, hop-off city tours aboard open-topped double-decker buses are a good way for Dubai first-timers to get their bearings. Buses with recorded commentary in several languages run on three interlinking routes, making 35 stops at major malls, beaches and landmarks. Passes also include extras such as a dhow cruise, a night bus tour and museums admissions. Tickets are sold online (10% discount), on the bus or at hotels. (☑04 340 7709; www.bigbustours.com; 24hr ticket adult/child US$69/41, 48hr US$73/47, one week US$83/54)

Wafi City
AREA

11 ⊙ MAP P56, C8

Ancient Egypt gets a Dubai-style makeover at this lavishly designed hotel, residential, restaurant and shopping complex, complete with pyramids, hieroglyphs and statues of Ramses and Anubis. The best time to visit is during the light and sound show that kicks off nightly at 9.30pm (September to May). In the cooler months, free outdoor movie screenings take over the Rooftop Gardens on Sunday nights at 8.30pm.

Wafi City was created in the 1990s and was one of the emirate's first new modern districts that combined entertainment, leisure, shopping and living. (☑04 324 4555; www.wafi.com; Oud Metha & Sheikh Rashid Rds; P; M Dubai Healthcare City)

Diwan Mosque
MOSQUE

12 ⊙ MAP P56, E2

The distinctive ornate flat dome and slender minaret of this snowy white mosque watch over the Al Fahidi Historic District (p52). Non-Muslims may only visit the interior on guided tours offered by the Sheikh Mohammed Centre for Cultural Understanding (p58). (Al Mussalah St; admission free; M Al Fahidi)

Eating

Arabian Tea House
CAFE $$

13 MAP P56, E2

A grand old tree, white wicker chairs, turquoise benches and billowing flowers create a sun-dappled refuge in the courtyard of an old pearl merchant's house. The menu includes lots of Emirati specialities, including *raqaq* (traditional bread), chicken *majboos* (spicy casserole with rice) and *saloona* chicken (in a tomato-based stew). (04 353 5071; www.arabianteahouse.co; Al Fahidi St; breakfast Dhs30-65, mains Dhs48-65; 7.30am-10pm; Al Fahidi)

Tomo
JAPANESE $$$

14 MAP P56, C8

The name of this gorgeously formal restaurant translates as 'long-time friend', which is quite apropos given its league of loyal followers. No gimmicky fusion here, just Japanese cuisine at its best: super-fresh sushi and sashimi, delectable Wagyu beef, feathery tempura and other treasured morsels. Plus dazzling views from the 360-degree terrace on the 17th floor of the Raffles Hotel. (04 357 7888; www.tomo.ae; 13th St, 17th fl, Raffles Hotel, Wafi City; mains Dhs70-550; 12.30-3.30pm & 6.30pm-1am; Dubai Healthcare City)

Sind Punjab
INDIAN $

15 MAP P56, D2

Like a fine wine, some restaurants only get better over time and such is the case with Sind Punjab, the first family eatery to open in Meena Bazaar in 1977. It still has a feverish local following for its finger-lickin' northern Indian specialities like butter chicken and *dal makhani* (a rich black-lentil and kidney-bean stew). (04 352 5058; cnr Al Esbij & 29A Sts; mains Dhs15-38; 8.30am-2am; Al Fahidi, Al Ghubaiba)

Al Ustad Special Kabab
IRANIAN $

16 MAP P56, E3

Sheikhs to shoe shiners clutter this funky, been-here-forever (since 1978, to be precise) kebab joint formerly known as Special Ostadi. Amid walls plastered with photographs of happy guests, a fleet of swift and quirky servers brings heaping plates of rice and yoghurt-marinated chicken into a dining room humming with chatter and laughter. (04 397 1933; Al Musallah Rd; mains Dhs25-42; noon-4pm & 6.30pm-1am Sat-Thu, 6.30pm-1am Fri; Al Fahidi)

Eric's
INDIAN $

17 MAP P56, D5

Prints by Goan cartoonist Mario Miranda decorate the simple, buzzing dining room of this purveyor of magically spiced dishes from the tropical Indian state of Goa. The menu has few false notes, but popular items include the chicken 'lollipops' (drumsticks), the Bombay duck (actually a fish!) and the chicken *xacuti*, a mouthwatering curry with poppy seeds. (04 396 5080; 10b St, Sheikh Hamdan Colony, Karama; mains Dhs20-40; 11.30am-3.30pm & 6.30pm-midnight; ; M BurJuman, ADCB)

Saravana Bhavan INDIAN $

18 MAP P56, E1

Head a block back from the Bur Dubai Abra Station to find this superb no-frills place, one of the best South Indian vegetarian restaurants in town. The vast menu includes wonderfully buttery *palak paneer*, creamy rogan josh, fragrant biryanis and other staples. Oddly, it also has a reputation for having excellent filter coffee! (04 353 9988; Khalifa bin Saeed Bldg, 3A St; mains Dhs15-17; 7am-11pm Sat-Wed, to 11.30pm Thu & Fri; ; M Al Ghubaiba)

Antique Bazaar INDIAN $$

19 MAP P56, E3

Resembling an exotic Mogul palace, Antique Bazaar's decor is sumptuously ornate with carved-wood seats, ivory-inset tables and richly patterned fabrics. Thumbs up to the *machli mirch ka salan* (fish with coconut, tamarind and curry) and the *gosht awadhi* biryani (rice with lamb, saffron and nuts). At dinnertime, a music and dance show competes with the

Arabian Tea House

Hitting Old Dubai's Food Trail

For a mouthwatering immersion in Dubai's multiethnic food and culture, book a small-group walking tour with Arva Ahmad of **Frying Pan Adventures** (www.fryingpanadventures.com; tours Dhs442). Enjoy five or six exotic nibbles from India, Lebanon or Nepal as either Arva or her sister Farida takes you through the bewildering tangle of Bur Dubai's or Deira's lanes while also feeding you tidbits about the food, the restaurants and local life. Check the website for the schedule and to book a tour.

food for your attention. (📞04 397 7444; www.antiquebazaar-dubai.com; Khalid bin al Waleed Rd, Four Points by Sheraton Bur Dubai, Mankhool; mains Dhs46-130; ⏲12.30am-3pm & 7.30pm-midnight; 🅿🛜; Ⓜ Al Fahidi)

Kabul Darbar
AFGHANI $

20 🍴 MAP P56, D2

Follow Afghan tradition: find a spot on the carpet, order lots of food and eat with your hands. All dishes are served with a soup, bread and salad, making for a filling and delicious meal. (📞04 325 0900; Khalid bin al Waleed Rd; mains Dhs20-40; ⏲noon-midnight Sat-Thu, 1pm-midnight Fri; Ⓜ Al Fahidi)

Govinda's
VEGETARIAN $

21 🍴 MAP P56, D4

Jains run this super-friendly, super-healthy vegetarian Indian restaurant serving 'body-harmonising' sattvic food that uses only fresh, seasonal and organic produce and shuns oil, onion and garlic. Dishes to try include the velvety *paneer makhanwala*

(Indian cheese in creamy tomato gravy) and the rich *dal makhani*. (📞04 396 0088; http://mygovindas. com; 4A St, Karama; mains Dhs30-42; ⏲noon-3.30pm & 7pm-midnight; 🍴; Ⓜ BurJuman)

Nepaliko Sagarmatha
NEPALI $

22 🍴 MAP P56, D2

At this small and basic joint, Nepali expats soothe their homesickness with platters of tasty *momos* (dumplings), including a version filled with 'buff' (buffalo), as well as steaming bowls of *thukpa* (noodle soup). It's a bit set back from the street overlooking a parking lot. (📞04 352 2124; Al Fahidi & 11th St; mains Dhs10-22; ⏲9am-midnight; Ⓜ Al Ghubaiba)

Vaibhav
INDIAN $

23 🍴 MAP P56, E2

This all-veg street food haven does a roaring trade in *dosas* (savoury wraps), stuffed *parathas* (pan-fried flatbread) and other southern Indian soul food, all prepared in a Bollywood-worthy spectacle. Try it with a cup of spicy masala chai (tea). Busiest at night. It hides out in a nondescript lane off Al Fahidi St opposite the Elegant Corner nuts store. It's behind the National Bank of Dubai. (📞04 353 8130; www.vaibhav.ae; Al Fahidi St; snacks Dhs2-20; ⏰7.30am-11pm; 🔊; Ⓜ Al Gubaibha)

Lebanese Village Restaurant
LEBANESE $

24 🍴 MAP P56, D3

At this tried-and-true eatery the best seats are under a shady umbrella on the pavement terrace (more appealing than the bright diner-style interior). The menu has few surprises, but does have staples like grills, hummus and *tabbouleh* (parsley, tomato and bulgar-wheat salad) dependably well. Also handy for takeaway if you're staying in a nearby hotel apartment. It's near the Ramada Hotel. (📞04 352 2522; Al Mankhool Rd; mains Dhs20-70; ⏰noon-2am; Ⓜ Al Fahidi)

Karachi Darbar
PAKISTANI $

25 🍴 MAP P56, C5

A favourite pit stop of expats and Karama Market (p69) shoppers with an eye for a biryani bargain, this local chain puts tummies into a state of contentment with a huge menu of Pakistani, Indian and Chinese dishes. Reliable picks include shrimp masala, mutton *kadai* and butter chicken. The chef can be a bit too generous with the ghee (clarified butter).

It's near Lulu Supermarket. (📞04 334 7272; 33B St, Karama Market; mains Dhs10-30; ⏰5am-2am; 🔊; Ⓜ ADCB)

Drinking

George & Dragon
PUB

26 🍺 MAP P56, E1

Keeping barflies boozy for a generation, this quintessential British dive comes with the requisite dartboard, pool table, greasy fish and chips, cheap beer and a painted window of St George jousting with the dragon. In the Ambassador, Dubai's oldest hotel (since 1971), it's fun, full of character(s) and a good place to wind down with a pint. (📞04 393 9444; www.astamb.com; Al Falah Rd, ground fl, Ambassador Hotel, Meena Bazaar; ⏰noon-3am; Ⓜ Al Ghubaiba)

Rock Bottom Café
PUB

27 🍺 MAP P56, D4

This been-here-forever Western expat fave has a '70s-era American roadhouse feel, with a cover band blaring out Top 40 hits and a DJ filling in the breaks with gusto. By day it's a regular cafe serving international soul food, but with a mob of friends and a bottle of tequila gone, it's the quintessential ending to a rollickin' night on the town. (📞04 396 3888; Sheikh Khalifa bin Zayed Rd, ground fl, Regent Palace Hotel, Karama; ⏰noon-3am; Ⓜ BurJuman)

Entertainment

Movies under the Stars

OUTDOOR CINEMA

28 MAP P56, C8

Every Sunday night during the cooler months, clued-in cinephiles invade the rooftop of the Pyramids Building, next to the Wafi Building, to drop into a giant beanbag and enjoy a free classic flick.

Food and nonalcoholic drinks are available. (☑04 324 4100; www.pyramidsrestaurantsatwafi.com; Pyramids Rooftop Gardens, Wafi City; admission free; ☺8.30pm Sun Feb-Apr; 🛜🚻; ⓂDubai Healthcare City)

Mini-Cruises

The **Dubai Ferry** (Map p56, E1; ☑800 9090; www.rta.ae; Shindagha Waterfront; adult/child Dhs50/25) provides a fun way for visitors to see the city from the water. Boats depart three times daily (11am, 1pm and 6.30pm) for the 90-minute trip from the Al Ghubaiba ferry station to the Dubai Marina station (and vice-versa). The route passes by such landmarks as Port Rashid, the Burj Al Arab and Madinat Jumeirah. Other options from either station include an afternoon-tea trip at 3pm and a sunset cruise at 5pm. The fare for any of these trips is Dhs50 (children Dhs25).

Shopping

BurJuman

MALL

29 🔒 MAP P56, D4

Rather than rest on its laurels, Dubai's oldest high-end mall (open since 1992) just keeps re-inventing itself. A recent remodel added some 200 shops (including luxury brands like Dior and Versace), a vast Carrefour supermarket and a 14-screen multiplex cinema. The upstairs food court, Pavilion Gardens, is an attractively designed, fountain-anchored space lidded by a soaring glass ceiling. (☑04 352 0222; www.burjuman.com; Sheikh Khalifa bin Zayed Rd; ☺10am-10pm Sat-Wed, to 11pm Thu & Fri; 🛜; ⓂBurJuman)

Wafi Mall

MALL

30 🔒 MAP P56, C8

At the heart of Egyptian-style Wafi City (p61) district, one of Dubai's most architecturally striking malls is built around three stained-glass pyramids and guarded by two giant statues of Ramses II. Stock up on gifts from around the Arabian world in the basement's **Souq Khan Murjan**, which was modelled after the namesake Baghdad bazaar. (☑04 324 4555; www.wafi.com; Oud Metha Rd; ☺10am-10pm Sat-Wed, to midnight Thu & Fri; 🛜; ⓂDubai Healthcare City)

Fabindia FASHION & ACCESSORIES

31 🔒 MAP P56, C2

In business since 1950, Fabindia is one of India's biggest retail chains and mostly sells products handmade by more than 50,000 Indian villagers using traditional skills and techniques. There's a huge selection of fashion, furnishings and handicrafts, including colourful *kurtis* (tunics), elegant shawls, patterned silk cushions and organic teas and chutneys, all at very reasonable prices. (☎04 398 9633; www.fabindia.com; Nashwan Bldg, Al Mankhool Rd; ◷10am-10pm Sat-Thu, 2-10pm Fri; Ⓜ ADCB)

Dubai Flea Market MARKET

32 🔒 MAP P56, B5

Trade malls for stalls and look for bargains amid the piles of preloved stuff that's spilled out of local closets at Dubai's cherished flea markets, which take place every weekend in a different spot around town, including at this great location inside the vast Zabeel Park. Check the website for upcoming markets. (☎055 886 8939; www. dubai-fleamarket.com; Gates 1 & 2, Zabeel Park; Dhs5; ◷8am-3pm every 1st Sat Oct-May; Ⓜ Al Jafiliya)

Ripe Market MARKET

33 🔒 MAP P56, B5

Held every Friday in beautiful Zabeel Park, this market features not only fruit and veg from local growers but also local honey, nuts, spices and eggs, plus arts and

Bacchanalian Boating

A memorable way to experience the magic of 'Old Dubai' is during a dinner cruise along the Creek. Gently cruise past historic waterfront houses, sparkling high-rises, jutting wind towers and dhows bound for India or Iran. Dining rooms are air-conditioned and alcohol is served. **Bateaux Dubai** (Map p56, F5; ☎04 814 5553; www.bateauxdubai.com; Baniyas Rd, near Emirates NBD; per person 2½hr dinner cruise with/without alcohol Dhs520/415, children Dhs190; ◷8.30-11pm; Ⓟ 🛜; Ⓜ Union) is a classy choice, especially if food is as important to you as ambience. Indulge in a four-course à la carte feast aboard this stylish contemporary boat with panoramic windows, linen-draped tables and live music.

crafts, food stations and locally roasted gourmet coffee – pretty much all you need for a picnic under the palms. (☎04 315 7000; http://ripeme.com/the-ripe-markets; Gate 2, Zabeel Park; ◷9am-2pm Fri late Oct-Mar; 🛜; Ⓜ Al Jafiliya)

Bateel FOOD

34 🔒 MAP P56, D4

Old-style traditional Arabian hospitality meant dates and camel milk. Now Emiratis offer their guests Bateel's scrumptious date chocolates and truffles, made using European chocolate-making techniques. Staff are happy to give you a sample before you buy. Most other Dubai malls have their own Bateel branches; check the website for details. (📞 04 355 2853; www.bateel.com; Sheikh Khalifa bin Zayed Rd, 1st fl, BurJuman Mall; 🕙10am-10pm Sun-Wed, to 11pm Thu & Fri; 🛜; Ⓜ BurJuman)

Ajmal PERFUME

35 🅰 MAP P56, D4

The place for traditional Arabian *attar* (perfumes), Ajmal custom blends its earthy scents and pours them into fancy gold or jewel-encrusted bottles. These aren't frilly French colognes – they're woody and pungent perfumes. Ask for the signature scent 'Ajmal',

based on white musk and jasmine. (📞 04 351 5505; www.ajmalperfume. com; Sheikh Khalifa bin Zayed Rd, Bur-Juman mall; 🕙10am-10pm Sat-Wed, to 11pm Thu & Fri; Ⓜ BurJuman)

Computer Plaza ELECTRONICS

36 🅰 MAP P56, D3

This jam-packed computer and electronics mall has more than 80 outlets selling every kind of computer hardware and accessory, including printers and scanners, plus software, mobile phones and cameras. On the ground floor, a handful of fast-food outlets and an ice-cream counter keep tummy rumblings in check. (📞 600 560 609, 055 335 5533; www.computer plaza-me.com; Al Mankhool Rd, Al Ain Center; 🕙10am-10pm Sat-Thu, 2-10pm Fri; Ⓜ Al Fahidi)

Attar (perfume) bottles

Karama Market

MARKET

37 🔒 MAP P56, C5

A visually unappealing concrete souq, Karama's bustling backstreet shopping area is crammed with shops selling handicrafts and souvenirs. Vendors may offer to take you to 'secret rooms' in the back of the building, which are crammed with knock-off designer bags and watches. (Karama Shopping Complex; www.facebook.com/karamaMarketDubai; 18B St; ⏰10am-10pm; Ⓜ️ADCB)

Dream Girl Tailors

CLOTHING

38 🔒 MAP P56, E2

Kamal Makhija and his army of tailors have had women looking good since 1971. They can create original designs, copy a beloved dress or even sew you an outfit from a magazine photo. (☎️04 388 0070; www.dreamgirltailors.com; Al Futtaim Bldg, 37D St, Meena Bazaar; ⏰10am-1pm & 4-10pm Sat-Thu, 6-9pm Fri; Ⓜ️Al Fahidi)

Hollywood Tailors

CLOTHING

39 🔒 MAP P56, E2

In business since 1976, this outfit specialises in men's suits and has lots of fabrics to choose from. Turn-around time ranges from three days to one week.

(☎️04 352 8551; http://hollywooduae.com; 37D St, Meena Bazaar; ⏰9.30am-1.30pm & 4-10pm Sat-Thu, 6-9pm Fri; Ⓜ️Al Fahidi)

The One

HOMEWARES

40 🔒 MAP P56, C8

Nirvana for design-minded home decorators, this airy showroom unites funky, innovative and top-quality items from dozens of international manufacturers. Even everyday items get a zany twist here, like pearl-beaded pillows, tiger-print wing-back chairs and vintage-style pendant lamps. (☎️600 541 007; www.theone.com; 1st fl, Wafi Mall; ⏰10am-10pm Sat-Wed, to midnight Thu & Fri; Ⓜ️Dubai Healthcare City)

Royal Saffron

SPICES

41 🔒 MAP P56, E2

This tiny shop tucked into the quiet lanes of Al Fahidi Historic District (p52) is a photogenic find. It's crammed full of spices like cloves, cardamom and cinnamon, plus fragrant oils, dried fruits and nuts, frankincense from Somalia and Oman, henna hair dye – and quirky salt and pepper sheikh and sheikhas. (☎️050 282 9565; Al Fahidi Historic District, Al Fahidi St; ⏰9am-9pm; Ⓜ️Al Fahidi)

Explore ◈
Jumeirah & Around

Dubai's answer to Bondi or Malibu, largely-residential Jumeirah stretches along the Arab Gulf from the Etihad Museum to the Burj Al Arab. In between are excellent public beaches, street art, urban lifestyle malls, boutique shopping and the new Dubai Canal that will reshape the district for years to come. New islands and peninsulas, meanwhile, continue to spring up offshore as well.

Surrounded by the turquoise Gulf, Jumeirah translates as 'the beautiful' and is synonymous with beaches. Its main drag is Jumeirah Rd which runs straight as a ruler parallel to the Gulf from the Etihad Museum in the north to the Burj Al Arab. Dubai may have perfected the mega-mall, but on Jumeirah Rd luxe indie boutiques and the compact Italian-style Mercato Mall rule. Near the museum, 2nd December St has some fine street art, while Jumeirah Mosque is one of few open to non-Muslims.

Bisected by the Dubai Canal, Jumeirah is largely a residential area, dominated by low-rise apartment buildings and white-washed villas. Although an older part of town, it has been injected with pockets of urban cool by several lifestyle malls along Al Wasl Rd as well as the sprawling City Walk development that's especially popular with Emirati hipsters and families.

Getting There & Around

Ⓜ Closest stops are **World Trade Centre**, **Emirates Tower**, **Financial Centre** and **Burj Khalifa/Dubai Mall**

🚗 Taxi to final destination

🚌 Bus 8 travels the entire length of Jumeirah Rd down to the Burj Al Arab.

Jumeirah Map on p72

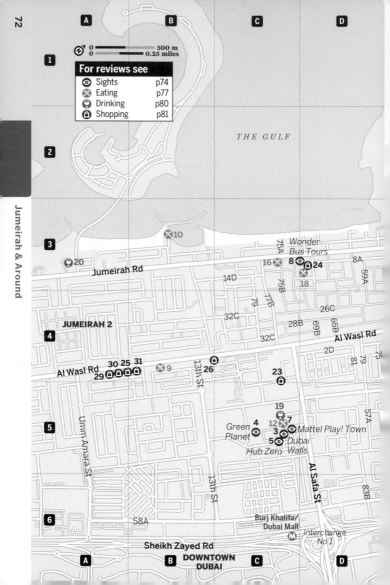

A **B** **C** **D**

1

0 ————— 500 m
0 ————— 0.25 miles

For reviews see
- 👁 Sights p74
- ❌ Eating p77
- 🍷 Drinking p80
- 🛍 Shopping p81

2

THE GULF

3

❌10

👁20   Wonder
Bus Tours
16❌ 8⊙ 🛍24
Jumeirah Rd   75A
14D   75B
18
79 77B   8A 59A
32C   79
28B 26C
JUMEIRAH 2   32C 28B 69B   Al Wasl Rd
4   2D   65B 75
30 25 31   81 79
Al Wasl Rd ❌9   23
29   13th St 🛍26   ⊙

5   19
Green 4 12❌7
Planet ⊙ 3⊙ Mattel Play! Town
5⊙ Dubai
Hub Zero Walls

Umm Amara St   13th St   57A

6   58A   Burj Khalifa/
Dubai Mall 83B
Sheikh Zayed Rd Ⓜ Interchange
No 1
**DOWNTOWN
DUBAI**

A **B** **C** **D**

E   F   G   H

1

2

3

4

5

6

6 ● Nikki Beach Dubai

22 ●● 21

● La Mer

27 🔒

2 ● Etihad Museum

1 ● Jumeirah Mosque
14 ●
28
11

Jumeirah Rd
17

2D
2D
6C

14A
45A
10D
19
16C
41A
20R
2C

35A
43A
18E
27B
25A
21E
6B
2C
11

JUMEIRAH 1

16B
20A
29
33
2B
6B
31
49
45
41
43A
35
39B

23
25B
24C
21B
27A
29
8B
12B
25
20D

9
16A
24B
10B
6B
2B
2A
10A
24A
3A
2A

Al Wasi Rd

17A
6A
9
8A
12A
14B
12A
16B
18B
20A
16A
18A

Al Huchaiba Rd

Satwa Roundabout
13 ●

15 ●

Dubai Street Museum

57A

Al Satwa Rd

6B
10B
18A
22B
32C

8A
6C
8C
12
19
20B
22A
22B
28A
30A
308

14A
18B
20A
11

2nd of December St

SATWA

Al Satwa Rd

12A
22A

2nd of December St

5

73B
308
19
57
15
11
5

Zabeel Roundabout

2nd Zabeel Rd

Sheikh Zayed Rd

M Emirates Towers

World Trade Centre
M

M Financial Centre
7
2
37
FINANCIAL CENTRE

17
21

E   F   G   H

Sights

Jumeirah Mosque MOSQUE

1 ◎ MAP P72, G3

Snowy white and intricately detailed, Jumeirah is Dubai's most beautiful mosque and one of only a handful in the UAE that are open to non-Muslims – one-hour guided tours are operated by the Sheikh Mohammed Centre for Cultural Understanding (p58). Tours conclude with pastries and a discussion session during which you're free to ask any question about Islam and Emirati culture. There's no need to book. Modest dress is preferred, but traditional clothing can be borrowed for free. Cameras are allowed. (📞04 353 6666; www.cultures.ae; Jumeirah Rd; tours Dhs20; ⏱tours 10am Sat-Thu; [P]; [M]Emirates Towers, World Trade Centre)

Etihad Museum MUSEUM

2 ◎ MAP P72, H3

Opened in January 2017, this striking modern museum engagingly chronicles the birth of the UAE in 1971, spurred by the discovery of oil in the 1950s and the withdrawal of the British in 1968. Documentary films, photographs, artefacts, timelines and interactive displays zero in on historic milestones in the years leading up to and immediately following this momentous occasion and pay homage to the country's seven founding fathers. Free tours of the adjacent circular Union House, where the agreement was signed, are available. (📞04 515 5771; http://etihadmuseum.dubaiculture.ae; Jumeirah St, Jumeirah 1; adult/child Dhs25/10; ⏱10am-8pm; [P]; [M]Al Jafiliya)

Dubai Walls PUBLIC ART

3 ◎ MAP P72, C5

More than a dozen hot shots of the international street-art scene, including Aiko, Blek Le Rat, ROA and Nick Walker, have turned new urban-style quarter City Walk into an outdoor gallery. The project was sponsored by City Walk developer Meraas. (City Walk; admission free; ⏱24hr; [M]Burj Khalifa/Dubai Mall)

Urban Art on 2nd December St

In 2016, 16 local and international street artists mounted their cherry-pickers to turn the rather drab facades on 2nd December St into the **Dubai Street Museum** (Map p72, H4; 2nd December St, Satwa; admission free; ⏱24hr; [M]Al Jafiliya), a striking outdoor gallery with murals reflecting Dubai's Bedouin heritage. Highlights include: *Emirati children* by French artist Seth Globepainter; *Resting Falcon* by Hua Tunan from China; *Founding Fathers* by Emirati artist Ashwaq Abdulla and *Old Man in Boat* by Russian artist Julia Volchkova.

Dome interior, Jumeirah Mosque

Green Planet
ZOO

4 ⊙ MAP P72, C5

If you can build a ski slope in the desert, why not a rainforest, too? In comes the Green Planet, an indoor tropical paradise intended to 'edutain' about biodiversity, nature and sustainability. More than 3000 animals and plants live beneath its green canopy, including birds, butterflies, frogs, spiders, snakes. The four-storey ecosystem is anchored by a giant fake tree covered in plants that will grow across it over time, making it look more like the real thing. (www.thegreenplanet dubai.com; City Walk, Al Madina St; adult/child Dhs95/70; ⊙10am-10pm Sat-Wed, 10am-midnight Thu & Fri; P; M Burj Khalifa/Dubai Mall)

Hub Zero
AMUSEMENT PARK

5 ⊙ MAP P72, C5

This high-tech indoor theme park is squarely aimed at getting serious gamers. Tickets buy access to 18 attractions, including a head-spinning VR experience, 3D dark rides, 4D cinema, race simulators, laser tag battles and a laser maze. The upper floor (free admission, pay as you go) has karaoke booths, pool tables and a 40-station area with the latest PC games. Nostalgic types can play retro games like Pac-Man and Space Invaders in the Time Warp Arcade. (☎800 637 227; www.hubzerodubai.com/en; City Walk, Jumeirah 1; master/hacker/child pass Dhs160/195/95; ⊙2-10pm Sat-Wed, to midnight Thu & Fri; P; M Burj Khalifa/Dubai Mall)

Dubai Canal

Water was released into the Dubai Canal (also called Dubai Water Canal) on 1 November 2016, marking the culmination of an amazing feat of engineering that connects the mouth of Dubai Creek with the Gulf. The Creek's first 2.2km extension created the Business Bay district and was completed in 2007. In December 2013, construction kicked off on the last 3.2km segment that cuts from Business Bay below Sheikh Zayed Rd and through Safa Park before spilling into the sea at Jumeirah Beach.

While office and hotel high-rises are being built at a frantic pace in Business Bay (including the edgy **Dubai Design District**; p112), the waterfront on the final stretch will be lined with residences, boutique hotels, cafes, marinas and other public spaces. A promenade conducive to jogging and walking parallels both banks. A highlight is the illuminated and motion-operated **waterfall** that cascades down both sides of Sheikh Zayed Bridge from 7pm to 10pm, stopping only for passing vessels. The **Dubai Ferry** runs several times daily from Al Jaddaf Marine Station at the mouth of Dubai Creek to Jumeirah.

Nikki Beach Dubai

BEACH

6 ◉ MAP P72, H1

At this fashionable pleasure pit on the emerging Pearl Jumeirah residential peninsula, only the crisp all-white look is virginal. On weekends, the bronzed, beautiful and cashed-up descend on the Dubai branch of the famous Miami beach club to frolic in the vast pool, lounge on daybeds, load up on seafood and toast the sunset with bubbly. Weekdays are quieter. (📞04 376 6162; www.nikkibeach.com/destinations/beach-clubs/dubai; Pearl Jumeirah Island; sun loungers weekdays/weekends Dhs150/300 with reservation; ⏰11am-9pm Sep-Jun; P; MAl Jafiliya)

Mattel Play! Town

PLAYGROUND

7 ◉ MAP P72, C5

In this adorable indoor playground, the milk-tooth brigade gets to build a house with Bob the Builder, put out fires with Fireman Sam, dance in front of a magic mirror with Angelina Ballerina and hang out with Barney and Thomas the Tank Engine. Parents, meanwhile, can nibble on a salad or lasagne at the **cafe**. (📞800 637 227; www.playtowndubai.com; City Walk; adult/child Dhs55/95; ⏰9am-6pm Sat-Wed, to 8pm Thu, 11am-8pm Fri; 🚻; MBurj Khalifa/Dubai Mall)

Wonder Bus Tours BOATING

8 MAP P72, C3

These unusual sightseeing tours have you boarding the bright yellow amphibious Wonder Bus at the Mercato Mall, driving down to the Creek, plunging into the water, cruising past historic Bur Dubai and Deira and returning to the shopping mall, all within the space of an hour. Tours run several times daily. (📞04 359 5656, 050 181 0553; http://wonderbusdubai.net; Mercato Mall, Jumeirah Rd, Jumeirah 1; adult/child 3-11yr Dhs170/120; Ⓜ BurJuman)

Eating

Logma FMIRATI $$

9 🍴 MAP P72, B4

Meaning 'mouthful' in Arabic, this funky Emirati cafe is a great introduction to contemporary local cuisine. It's popular for breakfast dishes such as *baith tamat* (saffron-spiced scrambled eggs with tomato), wholesome salads (try the pomegranate mozzarella) and sandwiches made with khameer bread. Swap your usual latte for sweet *karak chai* (spicy tea) – a local obsession – or a date shake. (📞800 56462; www.logma.ae; BoxPark, Al Wasl Rd, Jumeirah 1; mains Dhs60-70; 🕐8am-1am; 🛜🍽; 🚌12, 15, 93, Ⓜ Business Bay)

3 Fils ASIAN $$

10 🍴 MAP P72, B3

Singaporean chef Akmal Anuar turns out innovative, yet unpretentious Asian-influenced small plates at this tiny, unlicensed spot – a perfect foil to Dubai's expensive, overblown eateries. There are around 25 seats inside and a pint-sized kitchen in the corner, but try to nab one of the outside tables overlooking the bobbing yachts in the marina. Be sure to book at weekends. (📞056 273 0030; http://3fils.com; Jumeirah Fishing Harbour, Al Urouba St, Jumeirah 1; sharing plates Dhs22-75; 🕐1-11pm Mon-Wed, to midnight Thu-Sat; Ⓜ Burj Khalifa/Dubai Mall)

Vive La Mer

With shops, restaurants, a beachfront with hammocks and a huge playpark, **La Mer** (Map p72, F3; 📞800 637 227; www.lamerdubai. ae; Jumeirah 1; admission free; 🕐10am-midnight) is Dubai's newest beachfront destination. Still partly under construction (scheduled for completion in 2018), it's free to sunbathe or roam the complex. Kids will love the inflatable playground, and you're spoiled for choice when it comes to eating – try Motomachi for Japanese desserts or go local at Treej Cafe.

THE One Cafe
INTERNATIONAL $

11 MAP P72, G3

Deli dabblers will be in heaven at this stylish outpost upstairs at THE One home design store. All food is freshly prepared and calibrated to health- and waist-watchers without sacrificing a lick to the taste gods. Breakfast, including delicious eggs benedict, is served all day; (📞600 541 007; www.theone. com; Jumeirah Rd, Jumeirah 1; mains Dhs39-55; ⏰8am-8pm; ❄️🛜🚲; Ⓜ️World Trade Centre)

Lima Dubai
PERUVIAN $$$

12 MAP P72, C5

Dubai is no stranger to the Peruvian food craze, but when Michelin-starred Virgilio Martinez opened his outpost, it marked another milestone. The food here is a triumph of creative spicing and boldly paired ingredients. In one signature dish, braised octopus cuddles up to green lentils, potato cream and kalamata olives. Pair with an impeccable pisco sour, and you've got a mighty fine dinner. (📞056 500 4571; www.limadubai.com; City Walk, Jumeirah 1; mains Dhs90-200; ⏰noon-1am Sat-Tue, to 2am Wed-Fri; 🛜; Ⓜ️Burj Khalifa/Dubai Mall)

Ravi
PAKISTANI $

13 MAP P72, H4

Since 1978, everyone from cabbies to professional chefs has flocked to this Pakistani eatery, where you eat like a prince and pay like a pauper. Loosen your belt for heaping portions of grilled meats or succulent curries, including a few

Call to Prayer

While staying near a mosque, you'll most likely be woken up around 4.30am by the inimitable wailing of the *azan* (the Muslim call to prayer). There's a haunting beauty to the sound, one that you'll only hear in Islamic countries. Muslims pray five times a day: at dawn; when the sun is directly overhead; when the sun is in the position that creates shadows the same length as the object shadowed; at the beginning of sunset; and at twilight, when the last light of the sun disappears over the horizon. The exact times are printed in the daily newspapers and on websites. Muslims needn't be near a mosque to pray; they need only face Mecca. Those who cannot get to a mosque. may stop and pray wherever they are.

meatless option. Service is swift if perfunctory. Near the Satwa Roundabout. Cash only. (☑04 331 5353; Al Satwa Rd, Satwa; mains Dhs8-25; ⏲5am-2.30am; ☑; Ⓜ World Trade Centre)

Lime Tree Cafe
CAFE $

 14 ⊗ MAP P72, G3

This comfy Euro-style cafe is an expat favourite famous for its luscious cakes (especially the carrot cake), tasty breakfasts, creative sandwiches (stuffed into their homemade Turkish *pide*), roast chicken and pastas. It's located next to Spinneys. (☑04 325 6325; www.thelimetreecafe.com; Jumeirah Rd, Jumeirah 1; mains Dhs24-40; ⏲7.30am-6pm; 🛜☑; Ⓜ World Trade Centre)

Al Mallah
ARABIC $

15 ⊗ MAP P72, H4

Locals praise the chicken shawarma and fresh juices at this been-

here-forever traditional joint with shaded outdoor seating located on one of Dubai's most pleasant, liveliest and oldest walking streets. (☑04 398 4723; 2nd of December St, Satwa; sandwiches Dhs7-15; ⏲6am-2.30am; Ⓜ Al Jafiliya)

Al Fanar
EMIRATI $$

16 ⊗ MAP P72, C3

Al Fanar lays on the old-timey Emirati theme pretty thick with a Land Rover parked outside, a reed ceiling and waiters dressed in traditional garb. Give your tastebuds a workout with such local classics such as *majboos*, *saloona* or *harees* (porridge-like dish with meat). Breakfast is served all day. (☑04 344 2141; www.alfanarrestaurant.com; 1st fl, Town Center Mall, Jumeirah Rd, Jumeirah 1; mains Dhs42-68; ⏲noon-9.30pm Sun-Wed, to 10pm Thu, 9am-10pm Fri, to 9.30pm Sat; Ⓜ Burj Khalifa/Dubai Mall)

Comptoir 102
HEALTH FOOD $$

17 MAP P72, E3

In a pretty cottage with a quiet patio in back, this concept cafe comes attached to a concept boutique selling beautiful things for home and hearth. The daily changing menu rides the local-organic-seasonal wave and eschews gluten, sugar and dairy. There's also a big selection of vitamin-packed juices, smoothies and desserts. It's opposite Beach Centre mall. (☑04 385 4555; www. comptoir102.com; 102 Jumeirah Rd, Jumeirah 1; mains Dhs50-65, 3-course meal Dhs90; ⏱7.30am-9pm; 🛜⏱; Ⓜ Emirates Towers)

Ka'ak Al Manara
LEBANESE $

18 ❌ MAP P72, D3

Ka'ak is flat sesame bread that's a street-food staple in Lebanon. This upbeat mall-based eatery serves them with various sweet and savoury fillings, sprinkled with *zaatar* or sumac, and toasted just right. Try the classic picon cheese spread or a fusion special like the chicken fajita *ka'ak*. (☑04 258 2003; www.facebook.com/kaakalma nara; 1st fl, Mercato Mall, Jumeirah Rd, Jumeirah 1; dishes Dhs18-32; ⏱8.30am-midnight Sat-Wed, to 1am Thu & Fri; 🅿⏱; Ⓜ Burj Khalifa/ Dubai Mall)

Drinking

Grapeskin
WINE BAR

19 🚇 MAP P72, C5

At this stylish rustic wine bar imbued with a homey vibe you can match your wine to your mood. Most pours come from small vineyards and served with fine cheeses, meats and sharing platters. Chill to *sheesha* on the terrace or join the post-work expat crowd for happy hour between 6pm and 8pm. (☑04 403 3111; www.livelaville.com/dining/Grapeskin; La Ville Hotel & Suites, City Walk, Al Multaqa St, Jumeirah 1; ⏱4pm-1am Sun-Wed, 3pm-1am Thu-Sat; 🛜; Ⓜ Burj Khalifa/Dubai Mall)

Provocateur
CLUB

20 🚇 MAP P72, A3

At this ultra-posh party den, a well-heeled eye-candy crowd lolls on curved floral banquettes beneath an LED ceiling pulsating to a diverse beat bank, from edgy EDM to old-school hip-hop and R & B. Think tough door, smart-dress code, pricey drinks and top DJs. (☑055 211 8222, 04 343 8411; www. provocateurdubai.com; Four Seasons Resort, Jumeirah Rd, Jumeirah 1; ⏱11pm-3am Wed-Fri & Sun; Ⓜ Business Bay)

Buying Alcohol

One of the most common questions among first-time visitors is: 'Can I buy alcohol?' The answer is yes – in some places.

Tourists over 21 are allowed to drink alcohol in designated areas such as licensed bars and clubs attached to Western-style hotels. By law, drinking anywhere else does require being in possession of an alcohol licence which, however, is only issued to non-Muslim residents. The licence grants the right to purchase a fixed monthly limit of alcohol sold in special liquor stores such as African & Eastern and in some branches of Spinneys supermarket. Note that visitors are not officially permitted to purchase alcohol in these places, and staff are supposed to ask to see the licence.

When arriving by air, non-Muslim visitors over 18 may buy 4L of spirits, wine or beer in the airport duty-free shop. However, it is illegal to transport alcohol without a licence, whether in a taxi, rental car or the Dubai Metro. In practice, this is widely ignored.

Club Boudoir CLUB

21 MAP P72, G2

High on the glam-o-meter, Boudoir has been around the block once or twice but still pulls in beautiful punters with nights dedicated to hip-hop and R & B and others to *desi* (Bollywood music). (04 345 5995; www.clubboudoirdubai.com; Dubai Marine Beach Resort & Spa, Jumeirah Rd, Jumeirah 1; 10pm-3am; ; MWorld Trade Centre)

Sho Cho BAR, CLUB

22 MAP P72, G2

Although Sho Cho is primarily a Japanese restaurant, it's the heady lure of the cool Gulf breezes and potent cocktails on the laid-back terrace that continue to make this scene staple simply irresistible. (04 346 1111; www.sho-cho.com; Dubai Marine Beach Resort & Spa, Jumeirah Rd, Jumeirah 1; 7pm-3am Sun-Fri; ; MWorld Trade Centre, Emirates Towers)

Shopping

City Walk MALL

23 MAP P72, C4

Dubai's newest pedestrianised shopping, dining and entertainment district boasts urban-style streets and a contemporary glass-roofed mall. Along with more than 60 shops, 30-odd cafes and restaurants, and a 10-screen cinema complex, there is a handful of family-friendly attractions, including the Green Planet biodome and Hub Zero gaming centre. (www.citywalk.ae; Al Safa Rd; 10am-10pm; ; MBurj Khalifa/Dubai Mall)

Mercato Shopping Mall   MALL

24 🔒 MAP P72, D3

With 140 stores, Mercato may be small by Dubai standards, but it's distinguished by attractive architecture that looks like a fantasy blend of a classic train station and an Italian Renaissance town. Think vaulted glass roof, brick arches, a giant clock and a cafe-lined piazza. Retail-wise, you'll find upscale international brands and a Spinneys supermarket. (📞04 344 4161; www.mercatoshoppingmall.com; Jumeirah Rd, Jumeirah 1; ⏰10am-10pm; Ⓜ Financial Centre, Burj Khalifa/Dubai Mall)

BoxPark   SHOPPING CENTRE

25 🔒 MAP P72, A4

Inspired by the London original, this 1.3km-long outdoor lifestyle mall was built from upcycled shipping containers and has injected a welcome dose of urban cool into the Dubai shopping scene. The 220 units draw a hip crowd, including lots of locals, with quirky concept stores, eclectic cafes and restaurants and entertainment options including a cinema with on-demand screenings. (📞800 637 227; http://boxpark.ae; Al Wasl Rd; ⏰10am-midnight or later; 📶; Ⓜ Business Bay)

Galleria Mall   MALL

26 🔒 MAP P72, B4

The modern-Arabia design of this locally adored boutique mall is as much a draw as the shops, which include rare gems like the first

UAE branch of Saudi homeware store Cities and hip local fashions by Zayan. Wrap up a visit with a healthy lunch at South African cafe Tashas or gooey cakes from Emirati-owned Home Bakery. (📞04 344 4434; www.galleria-mall.ae; Al Wasl Rd; ⏰10am-midnight; Ⓜ Burj Khalifa/Dubai Mall)

S*uce   FASHION & ACCESSORIES

27 🔒 MAP P72, F3

Plain and simple they are not, the clothes and accessories at S*uce (pronounced 'sauce'), a pioneer in Dubai's growing lifestyle-fashion scene. Join fashionistas picking through regional and international designers and brands you probably won't find on your high street back home, including Alice McCall, Bleach and Fillyboo.

This is the original store. There are others in Dubai Mall, at The Beach at JBR and in the Galleria Mall. (📞04 344 7270; http://shopatsauce.com; ground fl, Village Mall, Jumeirah Rd; ⏰10am-10pm Sat-Thu, from 4pm Fri; Ⓜ Emirates Towers)

O Concept   FASHION & ACCESSORIES

28 🔒 MAP P72, G3

This Emirati-owned urban boutique-cum-cafe with shiny concrete floors and ducts wrapped in gold foil is a routine stop for fashionistas in search of up-to-the-second T-shirts, dresses, jeans and other casual-elegant fashions and accessories.

The cafe has delicious cappuccino and gluten-, sugar- and dairy-free desserts that actually taste good. (📞04 345 5557; www.facebook.com/Oconceptstore; Al Hudheiba Rd, Jumeirah 1; 🕙10am-10pm; 📶; Ⓜ World Trade Center)

Urbanist
HOMEWARES

29 🔒 MAP P72, A4

The Syrian couple behind Urbanist dedicate the store's shelf space to hand-curated items rooted in both tradition and modernity, Western and Middle Eastern tastes. None of the pieces – from tiny gold earrings to tunics and fez-shaped stools – are run of the mill. It's all displayed in a vibrant space where industrial cool meets antique cabinets and mother-of-pearl mirrors. (📞04 348 8002; www.facebook.com/Urbaniststore; Boxpark, Al Wasl Rd; 🕙10am-10pm Sun-Thu, to midnight Fri & Sat; Ⓜ Business Bay)

Typo
STATIONERY

30 🔒 MAP P72, A4

This is the kind of store where 'notebooks' are still made from paper. Indeed, here they come in all shapes and sizes, from cutesy

to corporate, along with lots of other fun but useful items like laptop bags, pencil cases and mobile phone covers.

There are several other branches around town, including Dubai Mall and Deira City Centre. (📞04 385 6631; http://typo.com; Boxpark, Al Wasl Rd; 🕙10am-10pm Sun-Thu, to midnight Thu & Fri; Ⓜ Business Bay)

Zoo Concept
GIFTS & SOUVENIRS

31 🔒 MAP P72, B4

This concept store in trendy Box-Park stocks quirky gifts, gadgets, jewellery, clothes and accessories. Owner Hussein Abdul Rasheed curates an always-interesting mix of up-and-coming local labels like Hudoob (pop culture caps) and international brands such as Retrosuperfuture sunglasses, alongside panda-printed plates and knitted Coco Chanel dolls.

There are also stores at Dubai Mall and Souk Al Bahar. (📞04 349 5585; Shop M08-01 BoxPark, Al Wasl Rd, Jumeirah 2; 🕙10am-10pm Sun-Thu, to midnight Fri & Sat; 📶; 🚌12, 15, 93, Ⓜ Burj Khalifa/Dubai Mall)

Explore ⊕
Burj Al Arab &
Madinat Jumeirah

The iconic Burj Al Arab is the star of this beautiful stretch of coast, also home to Madinat Jumeirah, a canal-laced 'Arabian Venice'. Away from the resorts, Kite and Sunset beaches are fabulous, while inland, shopping awaits at the Mall of the Emirates, which also shelters the surreal Ski Dubai indoor ski park.

If you're in town for a beach holiday, you won't find a finer stretch of sand than in around the Burj Al Arab, the famous superluxe resort and iconic symbol of Dubai's boom. Even if you're not staying in a fancy Gulf-adjacent hotel, you can frolic on public beaches offering everything from water-sports to global street-food treats. One stretch is even open at night for floodlit swims.

Want to shop in the souq but don't care for the dust, hubbub and haggling? At Souq Madinat Jumeirah you can bask in air-conditioned refinement while still soaking up Arabian Nights flair in its warren of narrow walkways shaded by carved wooden roofs. If you're more into mall-style shopping, head inland to the Mall of the Emirates to pick out some chic new threads and dip into the 'Alps in the Desert' at Ski Dubai.

Getting There & Around

Ⓜ For Burj Al Arab, Madinat Jumeirah and Sunset Beach: **Mall of the Emirates**

Ⓜ For Kite Beach: **Noor Bank**

🚗 Taxi to final destination

Burj Al Arab & Around Map on p92

Top Experience
Madinat Jumeirah

One of Dubai's most attractive developments, this resort is a contemporary version of a traditional Arab village, complete with a souq, palm-fringed waterways and desert-coloured villas festooned with wind towers. It's enchanting at night with romantically lit bougainvillea gardens and the Burj Al Arab gleaming in the background. At its heart lies Souk Madinat Jumeirah, a mazelike bazaar with shops lining wood-framed walkways and canalside restaurants.

◉ MAP P92, C3

☏ 04 366 8888

www.jumeirah.com

King Salman Bin Abdul Aziz Al Saud St, Umm Suqeim 3

Ⓜ Mall of the Emirates

Souq Madinat Jumeirah

Although the ambience at this maze-like **bazaar** (pictured; ☎04 366 8888; www.jumeirah.com; King Salman Bin Abdul Aziz Al Saud St, Umm Suqeim 3; ☉10am-11pm; 🛜) is too contrived to feel like an authentic Arabian market, the quality of some of the crafts, art and souvenirs is actually quite high. There are numerous cafes, bars and restaurant, the nicest of which overlook the waterways and the Burj Al Arab.

Abra Cruising

The desert seems far away as you glide past enchanting gardens of billowing bougainvillea, bushy banana trees and soaring palms on a 20-minute **cruise** (☎04 366 8888; www.jumeirah. com; Souk Madinat Jumeirah; adult/child Dhs85/50; ☉10am-11pm Nov-Apr, 11am-11pm May-Oct) aboard a traditional-style abra (wooden ferry). Tours leave from the Souk Madinat waterfront. No reservations are necessary.

Turtle Watching

The nonprofit **Dubai Turtle Rehabilitation Project** (www.facebook.com/turtle. rehabilitation) at the Jumeirah Al Naseem resort has nursed more than 560 injured or sick sea turtles back to health and released them into the Gulf. The turtles spend the last weeks before their release in the hotel's sea-fed lagoon, which can be visited daily. Feedings take place at 11am on Wednesdays.

Friday Brunch

Friday brunch is a time-honoured tradition, especially among Western expats. The Madinat hotels Al Qasr and Mina A'Salam are both famous for putting on a mindboggling cornucopia of delectables – from roast lamb and sushi to cooked-to-order seafood and beautiful salads.

★ **Top Tips**

o If you are staying at a Madinat hotel or eating at one of the restaurants, your abra shuttle is free.

o Make dinner or brunch reservations at least one week ahead for most of the restaurants.

o Take advantage of happy-hour deals offered at many Madinat bars.

o Maps are available at several information points.

✗ **Take a Break**

For sunset drinks with a view of the Burj Al Arab, the rug-lined terrace of the Bahri Bar (p98) is a perfect vantage point.

Book early for delicious seafood with Madinat and Burj Al Arab views at chic and sophisticated Pierchic (p96).

Top Sight

Burj Al Arab

When Dubai's ruler commissioned the Burj Al Arab in the 1990s, he gave architect Tom Wright a blank cheque to dream up an iconic structure that the entire world would associate with the tiny Gulf emirate. The final tally came to a $1.5 billion, but the gamble paid off: the Burj Al Arab's graceful silhouette, inspired by the billowing sail of a dhow, is as iconic to Dubai as the Eiffel Tower is to Paris.

⊙ MAP P92, D2

☎ 04 301 7777

www.burj-al-arab.com

off Jumeirah Rd, Umm Suqeim 3

Ⓜ Mall of the Emirates

Architecture & Design

The Burj has 60 floors spread over 321m and was the world's tallest hotel in the world at the time of its opening. British architect Tom Wright came up with the iconic design and signature translucent fibreglass facade that serves as a shield from the desert sun during the day and as a screen for the impressive illumination at night.

Interior

The Burj interior by British-Chinese designer Khuan Chew is every bit as over-the-top as the exterior is simple and elegant. The moment you step into the lofty lobby, a crescendo of gold-leaf, crystal chandeliers, hand-knotted carpets, water elements, pillars and other design elements put you on sensory overwhelm. Some of the 24,000 sq m of marble hail from the same quarry where Michelangelo got his material.

Optical Effect

The white metal crosspieces at the top of the Burj Al Arab form what is said to be the largest cross in the Middle East – but it's only visible from the sea. By the time this unexpected feature was discovered, it was too late to redesign the tower – the hotel had already put Dubai on the map and become the icon for the city. Go see the cross on a boat charter and decide for yourself. The scale is amazing.

Tea with a View

A cocktail or afternoon tea in this capsule-shaped **Skyview Bar** (🗲 04 301 7600; www. burjalarab.com; 🕑 1pm-2am Sat-Thu, from 7pm Fri) sticking out from the main building on the 27th floor is high on the to-do list of many Dubai visitors despite the steep minimum spends. Reservations are essential.

★ Top Tips

○ If you're not checking into the Burj, you need to make a reservation for cocktails, afternoon tea or a meal to get past lobby security (a minimum spend applies, the website has details).

○ For a surreal dining experience, book a table at Nathan Outlaw at Al Mahara (p97) to nosh on fish and seafood while seated before a giant, round aquarium.

✕ Take a Break

For romantic views of the Burj, head to the bars in Madinat Jumeirah, such as Bahri Bar (p98).

Watch the sun drop into the Gulf behind the Burj while sipping sundowners at perennially fashionable 360° (p98).

Walking Tour 🥾

Gallery Hopping Around Alserkal Avenue

*The most cutting-edge galleries within Dubai's growing art scene cluster in a sprawling warehouse campus called **Alserkal Avenue** (www.alserkal avenue.ae; 17th St, Al Quoz 1; M Noor Bank, FGB) in an industrial area called Al Quoz, east of Sheikh Zayed Rd. It's the brainchild of local developer and arts patron Abdelmonem bin Eisa Alserkal. A crop of urban cafes fuels the arty vibe.*

Walk Facts

Start Tom & Serg

End Salsali Private Museum

Length 3km; as long as you feel like admiring the galleries

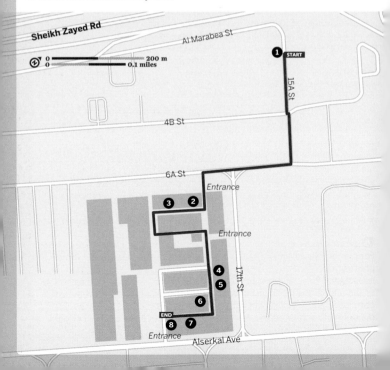

❶ Tom & Serg

Fuel up for your gallery hop at this lofty warehouse-style **cafe** (www.tomandserg.com; Al Joud Center, 15A St; mains Dhs37-79; ⏱8am-4pm Sun-Thu, to 6pm Fri & Sat; 🛜📶) with an open kitchen. The menu teems with feel-good food such as Moroccan chicken, eggs Benedict and a mean burger.

❷ The Third Line

The Third Line (www.thethirdline.com; Warehouse 78/80; ⏱10am-7pm Sat-Thu) has been a cornerstone of Dubai's growing gallery scene since 2005. It frequently introduces Emirati artists to collectors and art aficionados at such prestigious fairs as Art Basel.

❸ Mirzam Chocolate Makers

Mirzam (www.mirzam.com; Warehouse 70; ⏱10am-7pm Sat-Thu; 🚼) operates a 'Willy Wonka'–style factory where visitors can keep an eye on all stages of production – from roasting to hand-wrapping – taking place in a glass-encased chocolate laboratory. Drop by the integrated shop to sample and buy the final product. Staff also host free one-hour tasting workshops on weekends. Sign up via the website.

❹ Leila Heller Gallery

For over three decades, this prestigious New York **gallery** (www.leilahellergallery.com; Warehouse 87; ⏱10am-7pm Sat-Thu) has been a conduit for artistic and cultural dialogue between Western, Middle Eastern, Central Asian and Southeast Asian artists. Artists on its roster range include Tony Cragg and Pakistani artist Rashid Rana.

❺ Fridge

This talent management **agency** (www.thefridgedubai.com; Warehouse 5) runs a much-beloved concert series (usually on Fridays) that shines the spotlight on local talent still operating below the radar.

❻ Gallery Isabelle van den Eynde

This edgy **gallery** (www.ivde.net; Warehouse 17; ⏱10am-7pm Sat-Thu) has been a household name on the Dubai art scene since 2006. It promotes progressive and emerging talent from around the region and often presents envelope-pushing exhibits. Artists represented include Hassan Sharif and Bita Fayyazi.

❼ Ayyam Gallery

This **gallery's** (http://www.ayyamgallery.com; Unit D11; ⏱10am-6pm Sat-Thu) main mission is to promote emerging Middle Eastern artists and to introduce their often provocative, political and feminist work and voices to a wider audience.

❽ Salsali Private Museum

Ramin Salsali bought his first painting at 21 and has since grown his collection to comprise some 800 paintings, sculptures and installations. He presents a selection for free at this **private museum** (www.salsalipm.com; Warehouse 14; ⏱11am-4pm Sun-Thu) to inspire the next generation of art fans.

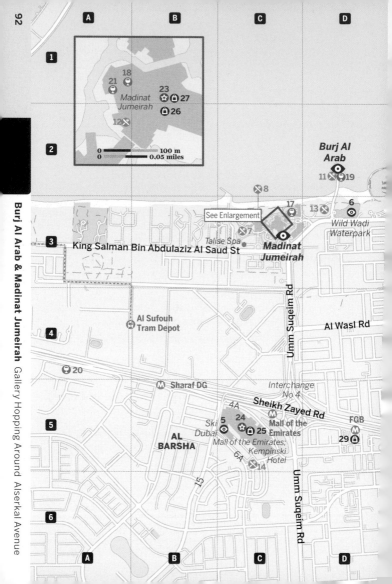

Burj Al Arab & Madinat Jumeirah Gallery Hopping Around Alserkal Avenue

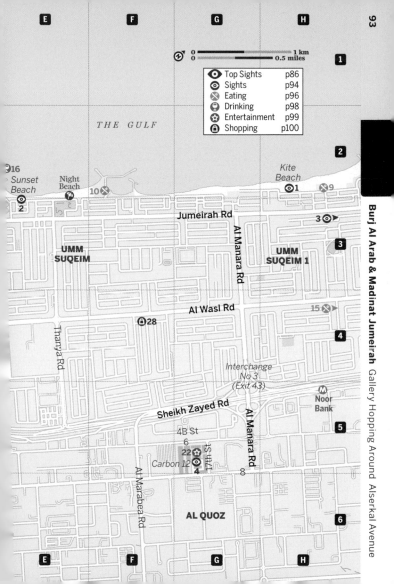

THE GULF

	Top Sights	p86
	Sights	p94
	Eating	p96
	Drinking	p98
	Entertainment	p99
	Shopping	p100

0 — 1 km
0 — 0.5 miles

E **F** **G** **H**

1

2

●16
Sunset
Beach
●2

Night
Beach
10

Kite
Beach
●1   9

Jumeirah Rd

3 ●

UMM
SUQEIM

Al Manara Rd

UMM
SUQEIM 1

3

Al Wasl Rd

15

28

4

Thanya Rd

Interchange
No 3
(Exit 43)

Noor
Bank

Sheikh Zayed Rd

Al Manara Rd

5

4B St
6
22
Carbon 12 ●
4

8

6

Al Marabea Rd

AL QUOZ

E **F** **G** **H**

Sights

Kite Beach
BEACH

1 ◎ MAP P92, H2

This long, pristine stretch of white sand, off Jumeirah Rd and next to a mosque, is superclean and has lots of activities, including kite surfing, soap football, beach tennis, beach volleyball and kayaking. There are showers, wi-fi, toilets and changing facilities, plus lots of food trucks and cafes. Great views of the Burj Al Arab. It gets very busy on Friday and Saturday when a seaside market with crafts and gifts sets up. (Sheikh Hamdan Beach; 2c St, off Jumeirah Rd, behind Saga World mall, Umm Suqeim 1; admission free; ☻sunrise-sunset; Ⓜ Noor Bank)

Sunset Beach
BEACH

2 ◎ MAP P92, E3

Just north of the Jumeirah Beach Hotel, Sunset is perfect for snapping that envy-inducing selfie with the Burj Al Arab as a backdrop. The wide, sandy strip has great infrastructure, including toilets, showers, changing cubicles and wi-fi via Smart Palms. There's also a short floodlit section for nighttime swimming.

Sunset is also Dubai's last surfing beach, with small to medium waves that are perfect for beginners. It's backed by tranquil Umm Suqeim Park, which has lawns and a playground. (Umm Suqeim Beach; Umm Suqeim 3; admission free; 👬; Ⓜ FGB, Mall of the Emirates)

Majlis Ghorfat Um Al Sheef
HISTORIC BUILDING

3 ◎ MAP P92, H3

This rare vestige of pre-oil times was built in 1955 as the summer retreat of Sheikh Rashid bin Saeed al Maktoum, the father of current ruler Sheikh Mohammed. The traditional two-storey gypsum-and-coral structure sports a palm-frond roof, a wind tower and window shutters carved from East African timber. The rug-lined *majlis* itself is decorated with rifles, daggers, coffee pots, radios and clocks and offers a glimpse into royal leisure living. The palm garden features a traditional *falaj* irrigation system. (☎ 04 226 0286; near Al Mehemal & Al Bagaara Sts, Jumeirah 3; adult/child Dhs3/1; ☻7.30am-2.30pm Sun-Thu; Ⓜ Business Bay, Noor Bank)

Carbon 12
GALLERY

4 ◎ MAP P92, G5

This minimalist white-cube space serves as a gateway to the UAE art scene for accomplished artists from around the world, and vice-versa. Some of them have roots in the Middle East, such as Tehran-born New York resident Sara Rahbar, whose textile art has made it into the British Museum. (☎ 04 340 6016; www.carbon12dubai. com; Warehouse 37, Alserkal Avenue, Al Quoz 1; ☻11.30am-7pm Sat-Thu; Ⓜ Noor Bank, FGB)

Ski Dubai

SKIING

5 MAP P92, C5

Picture this: it's 45°C outside, and you're wearing gloves and a hat and riding a chairlift through a faux alpine winter wonderland. Skiing in the desert? No problem. In Dubai, that is. Ski Dubai has delighted everyone from slope-starved expats to curious tourists and snow virgins since opening in 2005 as the first indoor ski park in the Middle East. (☏toll free 800 386; www.theplaymania.com/skidubai; Mall of the Emirates, Sheikh Zayed Rd, Al Barsha; slope day pass adult/child Dhs310/285, snow park Dhs210; ⊙10am-11pm Sun-Wed, 10am-midnight Thu, 9am-midnight Fri, to 11pm Sat; 👫; MMall of the Emirates)

Wild Wadi Waterpark

WATER PARK

6 MAP P92, D3

It's liquid thrills galore at Wild Wadi, where you can ride a water roller coaster (Master Blaster), plunge down a death-defying tandem slide (Jumeirah Sceirah) and get tossed around watery tornadoes (Tantrum Alley). Mellow types can chill on the lazy river while kids love romping around a vast water playground with smaller slides, water guns and a dumping bucket. (☏04 348 4444; www.wildwadi.com; Jumeirah Rd, Jumeirah 3; over/under 110cm tall Dhs310/260; ⊙10am-6pm Nov-Feb, to 7pm Mar-Oct; 👫; MMall of the Emirates)

Burj Al Arab & Madinat Jumeirah Sights

Sunset Beach

Night Beach

Fancy a night-time swim with the twinkling Burj Al Arab as a backdrop? Since May 2017, you can legally take a post-sunset dip along a 125m stretch of **beach** (Map p92, E2; Umm Suqeim 1 Beach; admission free; ⌚sunset-midnight; MFGB) illuminated by 12m-high wind- and solar-powered floodlights ('Smart Power Poles') and staffed with lifeguards. Find it about 1km north of the iconic landmark.

Eating

Pai Thai
THAI $$$

7 ✪ MAP P92, C3

An abra ride, a canalside table and candlelight are the hallmarks of a romantic night out, and this enchanting spot sparks on all cylinders. If your date doesn't make you swoon, then such expertly seasoned Thai dishes as wok-fried seafood and steamed sea bass should still ensure an unforgettable evening. Early reservations advised. (🕿04 432 3232; www.jumeirah.com; Madinat Jumeirah, King Salman Bin Abdul Aziz Al Saud St, Umm Suqeim 3; mains Dhs55-175; ⌚12.30-2.15pm Fri & Sat, 6-11.15pm; 🛜; MMall of the Emirates)

Pierchic
SEAFOOD $$$

8 ✪ MAP P92, C2

Looking for a place to drop an engagement ring into a glass of champagne? Make reservations (far in advance) at this impossibly romantic seafood house capping a historic wooden pier with front-row views of the Burj Al Arab and Madinat Jumeirah. The menu is a foodie's dream, with a plethora of beautifully prepared dishes. (🕿04 432 3232; www.jumeirah.com; Madinat Jumeirah, King Salman Bin Abdul Aziz Al Saud St, Umm Suqeim 3; mains Dhs125-450; ⌚12.30-3pm Sat-Thu & 6-11pm Sat-Wed, to 11.30 Thu & Fri; 🛜; MMall of the Emirates)

Salt
BURGERS $

9 ✪ MAP P92, H2

Salt started life as a roaming food truck serving delicious mini-burgers, before graduating to two silver Airstreams parked permanently at Kite Beach. Join the ever-present queue to place your order and then pull up some pallet furniture set right on the sand (or inside the air-conditioned glass cube, if the sun is starting to bite). (www.find-salt.com; 2C St, Kite Beach, Umm Suqeim 1; sliders Dhs30-50; ⌚11am-2am; 🛜; MNoor Bank)

Bu Qtair
SEAFOOD $$

10 ✪ MAP P92, F2

Always packed to the gills, this simple eatery is a Dubai institution famous for its dock-fresh fish and shrimp, marinated in a 'secret' masala curry sauce and fried to order. Belly up to the window, point to what you'd like and wait (about 30 minutes) for your order to be delivered to your table. Meals are priced by weight. (☑055 705 2130; off 2b St, Umm Suqeim Fishing Harbour, Umm Suqeim 1; meals Dhs40-125; ☺noon-11.30pm; P; MNoor Bank, FGB)

Nathan Outlaw at Al Mahara
SEAFOOD $$$

11 ⊗ MAP P92, D2

A lift posing as a submarine drops you into a gold-leaf-clad tunnel spilling into one of Dubai's most extravagant restaurants. Tables orbit a circular floor-to-ceiling aquarium where clownfish flit and baby sharks dart as their turbot and monkfish cousins are being devoured. Only the finest seafood imported from the UK – and prepared with deft simplicity – makes it onto plates here.

Dress code is enforced, and no children under 12 for dinner. (☑04 301 7600; http://almaharadubai.com; 1st fl, Burj Al Arab, Umm Suqeim 3; mains Dhs240-500, tasting menu Dhs950; ☺12.30-3.30pm, 7-11.30pm; P☎)

The Meat Co
STEAK $$$

12 ⊗ MAP P92, A2

Surrender helplessly to your inner carnivore at this canalside meat temple where yummy cuts of aged steaks range from Australian grain-fed Angus to New Zealand grass-fed beast, all available in small (200g) and large (300g) portions. Book ahead for a canalside table with Burj Al Arab view or hide out in the dark-wood dining room. (☑04 368 6040; www.themeatco.com; Souq Madinat Jumeirah, King Salman Bin Abdul Aziz Al Saud St, Umm Suqeim 3; mains Dhs165-390; ☺noon-11.45pm Sat-Wed, to 12.30am Thu & Fri; P☎; MMall of the Emirates)

Rockfish
SEAFOOD $$$

13 ⊗ MAP P92, D3

With silver-and-white interiors and a sandy terrace with front-row views of Burj Al Arab, Rockfish serves up Mediterranean-style seafood in glam but unstuffy surroundings. The compact menu kicks off with *crudo* (raw seafood), moves on to salads and soups, and reaches a crescendo with piscine treats laced with Arabic influences. (☑04 366 7640; www.jumeirah.com; Jumeirah Al Naseem, King Salman Bin Abdul Aziz Al Saud St, Umm Suqeim 3; mains Dhs65-175; ☺8-11am, 12.30-3.30pm, 6.30-11.30pm; P☎; ☒81, MMall of the Emirates)

Al Amoor Express
EGYPTIAN $

14 ⊗ MAP P92, C5

Vintage black-and-white photos of Egyptian actors keep an eye on diners here for their *koshari* fix (rice, macaroni and lentil 'porridge'), although it's more fun to order one of their famous cheese-, vegetable- or meat-stuffed *feteer* pies and watch the baker sling and whirl the dough behind the counter.

The falafel also gets our thumbs up. (📞04 347 0787; Halim St, Al Barsha 1; mains Dhs10-56; ⏱7.30am-2am; Ⓜ Mall of the Emirates)

BookMunch Cafe

CAFE $

15 🍽 MAP P92, H4

Literati young and old love this adorable bookstore-cafe combo geared toward families. It not only has a fabulous selection of children's books in several languages but also a progressive menu sure to please both tots and grown-ups. Menu stars include ginger-chilli-caramel shrimp, strawberry-kale salad and grandma's tarte tatin, and breakfast is served all day. (📞04 388 4006; www.bookmunch-cafe.com; Al Wasl Sq, Al Wasl Rd; mains Dhs38-68; ⏱7.30am-10pm Sun-Wed, 8am-10.30pm Thu-Sat; 🛜🚼; Ⓜ Business Bay)

Drinking

360°

LOUNGE

16 🚇 MAP P92, E2

Capping a long curved pier, this fashionable lounge still hasn't lost its cool after many years of music, mingling and magical views of the Burj Al Arab. Hang out on the deck or head inside to nibble on pan-Asian bites. On weekends top-notch DJs spin house for shiny, happy hotties; other nights are mellower. Must be 21 (ID required). (📞reservations 055 500 8518; www.jumeirah.com; Jumeirah Rd, Umm Suqeim 3; ⏱5pm-3am; 🛜; Ⓜ Mall of the Emirates)

Bahri Bar

BAR

17 🚇 MAP P92, C3

This chic bar drips with sultry Arabian decor and has a verandah laid with Persian rugs and comfy sofas perfect for taking in magical views of the Madinat waterways and the Burj Al Arab. Daily drink deals, elevated bar bites, and bands or DJs playing jazz and soul make the place a perennial fave among locals and visitors. (📞04 432 3232; www.jumeirah.com; Mina A'Salam, Madinat Jumeirah, King Salman Bin Abdul Aziz Al Saud St, Umm Suqeim 3; ⏱4pm-2am Sat-Wed, to 3am Thu & Fri; 🛜; Ⓜ Mall of the Emirates)

Agency

WINE BAR

18 🚇 MAP P92, A1

There aren't many bars dedicated to wine in Dubai, but Agency has held a pole position for quite some time. Overlooking the Madinat canals and decked out in dark wood and red velvet, it's home to one of the city's best day-time happy hours, offering drinks from Dhs25 and entire bottles of wine from Dhs100 between noon and 8pm. (📞04 366 5845; www.jumeirah.com; Souk Madinat Jumeirah, King Salman Bin Abdul Aziz Al Saud St, Umm Suqeim 3; ⏱noon-1pm; 🛜; Ⓜ Mall of the Emirates)

Gold on 27

COCKTAIL BAR

19 🚇 MAP P92, D2

Signature cocktails at this gold-dipped bar on the 27th floor of the Burj Al Arab are crafted with local lore or landmarks in mind and often featuring surprise ingredients. The whisky-based Light Sweet Crude, for instance, also contains a smidgeon of foie gras and charcoal-infused truffle oil. Prices are as sky-high as the location and reservations are essential. (📞04 301 7600; www.goldon27.com; Burj Al Arab, Umm Suqeim 3; ⏰6pm-2am; 📶; Ⓜ Mall of the Emirates)

Casa Latina
BAR

20 🚇 MAP P92, A4

With its alt-vibe, candle-lit booths and inexpensive drinks, this Cuban-themed bar attracts a non-poser crowd that's more into the music than looking good. It also hosts two of the most happening monthly parties, the punk-indie-eclectic Bad House Party and the awesome Bassworx drum and bass session. Happy hour from 6pm to 8pm. (📞04 399 6699; www.facebook.com/pg/Casalatinaofficialpage; ground fl, Ibis Hotel Al Barsha, Sheikh Zayed Rd, Al Barsha 1; ⏰6pm-2am; 📶; Ⓜ Sharaf DG)

Folly by Nick & Scott
BAR

21 🚇 MAP P92, A1

This sprawling multistorey venue has a woodsy interior with an open kitchen, but it's really the three bars with killer views of the Burj Al Arab that steal the show. It's the latest venture by Nick Alvis and Scott Price, so expect quality nibbles (Dhs45 to Dhs110) to go with your cocktails, beer or biodynamic wines. (📞04

430 8535; www.facebook.com/follydubai; Souk Madinat Jumeirah, King Salman Bin Abdul Aziz Al Saud St, Umm Suqeim 3; ⏰noon-2.30pm & 5-11pm Sun-Thu, noon-3.30pm & 5-11pm Fri & Sat; 📶; Ⓜ Mall of the Emirates)

Entertainment

Cinema Akil
CINEMA

22 ⭐ MAP P92, G5

Treating cineastes to smart indie flicks from around the world on a pop-up basis since 2014, this dynamic platform has now taken up permanent residence at the Alserkal Avenue. Screenings are often followed by Q&A sessions with directors. (www.cinemaakil.com; Alserkal Avenue, Al Quoz 1)

Yoga on the Beach

Downward dog and sun salutation with a view of the Burj Al Arab? Just sign up for the daily sunset yoga sessions (Dhs90) organised by the on-site **Talise Spa** (Map p92, C3; 📞04 366 6818; www.jumeirah.com; Al Qasr Hotel, Madinat Jumeirah; ⏰9am-10pm; Ⓜ Mall of the Emirates) and on Madinat Jumeirah's private beach. An even more spiritual journey awaits during Full Moon Yoga (Dhs99) – if you can get the timing right.

Madinat Theatre

THEATRE

23 MAP P92, B1

The program at this handsome 442-seat theatre at Souk Madinat is largely calibrated to the cultural cravings of British expats. Expect plenty of crowd-pleasing entertainment ranging from popular West End imports to stand-up comedy, toe-tapping musicals, Russian ballet and kids' shows. (📞04 366 6546; www.madinattheatre.com; Souq Madinat Jumeirah, King Salman Bin Abdul Aziz Al Saud St, Umm Suqeim 3; Ⓜ Mall of the Emirates)

Dubai Community Theatre & Arts Centre

THEATRE

24 MAP P92, C5

This thriving cultural venue puts on all sorts of global diversions, from Shakespeare and classical concerts to Bollywood musicals, Arabic folklore and art exhibits. Much support is given to Emirati talent, making this a good place to keep tabs on the local scene. (DUCTAC; 📞04 341 4777; www.ductac. org; 2nd level, Mall of the Emirates, Sheikh Zayed Rd, Al Barsha; ◷9am-10pm Sat-Thu, 2-10pm Fri; Ⓜ Mall of the Emirates)

Shopping

Mall of the Emirates

MALL

25 MAP P92, C5

Home to Ski Dubai (p95), a community theatre, a 24-screen multiplex cinema and – let's not forget – 630 stores, MoE is one of Dubai's most popular malls. With narrow walkways and no daylight, it can feel a tad claustrophobic at peak times (except in the striking Fashion Dome, lidded by a vaulted glass ceiling and home to luxury brands). (📞04 409 9000; www. malloftheemirates.com; Sheikh Zayed Rd, Al Barsha; ◷10am-10pm Sun-Wed, to midnight Thu-Sat; 📶; Ⓜ Mall of the Emirates)

Camel Company

GIFTS & SOUVENIRS

26 MAP P92, B2

Hands-down the best spot for kid-friendly camel souvenirs: stuffed camels in all sizes and colours, camels on T-shirts, coffee cups, notebooks, greeting cards, fridge magnets – if you can slap a camel on it, Camel Company has done it. (📞04 368 6048; www.camelcompany. ae; Souk Madinat Jumeirah, King Salman Bin Abdul Aziz Al Saud St, Umm Suqeim 3; ◷10am-11pm; 📶; Ⓜ Mall of the Emirates)

Jalabiyat Yasmine

FASHION & ACCESSORIES

27 MAP P92, B1

This small boutique specialises in *jalabiyas* (traditional kaftans native to the Gulf) and other Arabic fashion, although most visitors will likely be drawn in by its huge selection of elegantly patterned shawls. The finest are handmade by weavers in Kashmir from genuine pashmina (cashmere)

Pashmina: Telling Real from Fake

Pashmina shawls come in all sorts of wonderful colours and patterns. Originally made from feather-light cashmere, there are now many cheaper machine-made synthetic versions around. Before forking over hundreds of dirham, how can you make sure you're buying the real thing? Here's the trick. Hold the fabric at its corner. Loop your index finger around it and squeeze hard. Now pull the fabric through. If it's polyester, it won't budge. If it's cashmere, it'll pull through – though the friction may give you a mild case of rope burn. Try it at home with a thin piece of polyester before you hit the shops and then try it with cashmere. You'll never be fooled again.

or shahtoosh (the down hair of a Tibetan antelope). Machine-made shawls start at Dhs150. (☏04 368 6115; www.jalabiyasmine.com; Souk Madinat Jumeirah, King Salman Din Abdul Aziz Al Saud St, Umm Suqeim 3; ◷10am-11pm; Ⓜ Mall of the Emirates)

O' de Rose   FASHION & ACCESSORIES

28 🔒 MAP P92, F4

Enjoy a sip of rose water upon entering this quirky concept boutique run by a trio of free-spirited cousins from Beirut. They share a passion for unusual things, as reflected in the store's eclectic line-up of ethnic-chic clothing, accessories, and art and home decor, most of it created by indie designers from around the region.

(☏04 348 7990; www.o-derose. com; 999 Al Wasl Rd, Umm Suqeim 2; ◷10am-8pm Sat-Thu; Ⓜ Noor Bank, FGB)

Gold & Diamond Park   JEWELLERY

29 🔒 MAP P92, D5

An air-conditioned, less atmospheric alternative to the Deira Gold Souq, this buttoned-up business mall houses some 90 purveyors of bling. No bargaining here. If you can't find what you want, it's possible to commission a bespoke piece and have it ready in a couple of days. Refuel at the cafes ringing an outdoor courtyard. (☏04 362 7777; www.goldanddiamondpark.com; Sheikh Zayed Rd; ◷10am-10pm Sat-Thu, 4-10pm Fri; Ⓜ FGB)

Explore

Downtown Dubai

Dubai's vibrant centre is anchored by the 828m-high Burj Khalifa, the world's tallest structure, and brims with futuristic architecture, especially along Sheikh Zayed Rd and in the Dubai Design District. Downtown sights include the Dubai Mall, the Dubai Fountain and the Dubai Opera. The Dubai Canal cuts through Business Bay before spilling into the Gulf.

The Burj Khalifa overlooks the Dubai Mall, the world's biggest shopping temple with 1200 shops and attractions such as a three-storey aquarium, an ice rink and a dinosaur skeleton. Next door is the mesmerising Dubai Fountain with choreographed dance, music and light shows nightly. There are also good views from the rooftop of the striking new Dubai Opera.

To tap into Dubai's creative scene, swing by the emerging Dubai Design District or head straight to the hip Alserkal Avenue complex. In the industrial district of Al Quoz, the latter is a cluster of warehouses-turned-art campus with cutting-edge galleries alongside hipster cafes, a community theatre, a chocolate factory, arthouse cinema and other creative enterprises. For more regional art, scan the prestigious galleries at Gate Village at the monumental Dubai International Financial Centre.

Getting There & Around

Dubai Metro's Red Line runs the entire length of Sheikh Zayed Rd.

Ⓜ **Financial Centre / Emirates Towers / Burj Khalifa / Dubai Mall / Noor Bank / FGB**

Downtown Dubai Map on p108

Aerial view of Downtown Dubai NIKADA/GETTY IMAGES ©

Top Sight 🔭
Burj Khalifa

The Burj Khalifa is a ground-breaking feat of architecture and engineering with two observation decks on the 124th and 148th floors as well as the At.mosphere restaurant-bar on the 122nd. The world's tallest building pierces the sky at 828m (seven times the height of Big Ben); it opened in 2010, and only took six years to build. Up to 13,000 workers toiled day and night, putting up a new floor in as little as three days.

◉ MAP P108, D3

📞 800 2884 3867

www.atthetop.ae

1 Mohammed bin Rashid Blvd, entry LG, Dubai Mall

🚻

Ⓜ Burj Khalifa/Dubai Mall

Construction

Engineers and the Chicago-based architectural firm Skidmore, Owings & Merrill (SOM) had to pull out all the stops in the construction of the Burj Khalifa. Pouring the 11.5 feet (3.5m) thick foundation alone required 16,350 cubic yards (12,500 cubic metres) of reinforced concrete. The design was inspired by a the *Hymenocallis* desert lily.

At the Top Observation Deck

Taking in the views from the world's tallest building is a deservedly crave-worthy experience and a trip to the **At the Top** observation deck (pictured; 452m) on the 124th floor (adult/child 4-12yr Dhs125/95 non-prime hours, Dhs200/160 prime hours; ☺8.30am-11pm; Last entry 45min before closing) is the most popular way to do it. Use high-powered 'viewfinders' that bring even distant developments into focus (at least on clear days) and cleverly simulate the same view at night and in the 1980s. In addition, digital telescopes with HD cameras zero in on places outside the cityscape. Getting to the deck means passing various multimedia exhibits until a double-decker lift zips you up at 10m per second.

At the Top Sky

To truly be on the world's highest observation platform (555m), though, you need to buy tickets to **At the Top Sky** (non-prime/prime hours Dhs350/500, audioguide Dhs25; ☺11am-10pm). A visit here is set up like a hosted VIP experience with refreshments, a guided tour and an interactive screen where you 'fly' to different city landmarks by hovering your hands over high-tech sensors. Afterwards, you're escorted to the 125th floor to be showered with Burj trivia and take in another attraction called 'A Falcon's Eye View' that lets you take a virtual flight over the emirate by soaring over key attractions like a bird.

★ **Top Tips**

❍ Timed tickets are available at the ticket counter and often sell out quickly. Better to book online up to 30 days in advance.

❍ Book especially early if you want to go up at sunset.

❍ On hazy days, it's better to visit at night.

❍ Budget at least two hours for your visit.

❍ No refunds or rain checks are given if the outdoor viewing terrace is closed for bad weather.

❍ Prices go up during prime hours (around sunset) and closing times may vary depending on demand and the season.

✖ **Take a Break**

For fresh organic salads and mains with a view of the Burj and the lake, head to Baker & Spice (p112).

Top Sight 🛍
Dubai Mall

The 'mother of all malls' is much more than the sum of its 1200 stores: it's a village-sized family entertainment centre with a three-storey aquarium, a genuine dinosaur skeleton, indoor theme parks, state-of-the-art cinemas and an Olympic-sized ice rink. It also boasts a pretty souq and a designer fashion avenue with catwalk. Over than 150 food outlets to provide sustenance, some with outside terraces for front-row views of the Dubai Fountain and the Burj Khalifa.

◎ MAP P108, D3

📞 800-382 246 255

www.thedubaimall.com

Sheikh Mohammed bin Rashid Blvd

🕙 10am–midnight

🛜 🚻

Ⓜ Burj Khalifa/Dubai Mall

Dubai Fountain

In a lake flanked by the Burj Khalifa and Dubai Mall, these spectacular dancing **fountains** (https://thedubaimall.com/en/entertain-detail/the-dubai-fountain-1; Burj Lake; admission free; ⏱shows 1pm & 1.30pm Sat-Thu, 1.30pm & 2pm Fri, every 30min 6-11pm daily) elicit oohs and aahs from young and old and are especially impressive after dark. Jets shooting up to 140m high are choreographed to move to a rotating roster of Western, Arabic and classical rhythms. The viewing area outside the Dubai Mall usually gets jam-packed. Tip: reserve a terrace table at one of restaurants here or in Souk Al Bahar.

Dubai Aquarium & Underwater Zoo

About 75cm of plexiglass separates the rays, sharks, clownfish, groupers and around 250 other species of this **aquarium** (www.thedubaiaquarium.com; ground fl, Dubai Mall; packages Dhs100-300; ⏱10am-11pm Sun-Wed, to midnight Thu-Sat; P🚻) from its visitors. Three storeys high and in the middle of the mall, the giant tank (pictured) recreates an underwater habitat complete with artificial coral reefs and rocks. It's free to view from outside but you'll need tickets to access the walk-through tunnel and the upstairs Underwater Zoo where you can pay your respect to King Croc, a 5.1m-long crocodile, and his companion, Queen Croc.

Dubai Dino

Dubai's oldest denizen could hardly have imagined that he would make the trip from Wyoming to the Gulf some 155 million years after his death. Unearthed in 2008, the 24m-long and 7.6m-high dinosaur skeleton has held court among the sweeping arches of the Souk Dome since 2014.

★ Top Tips

o Pick up a map and store directory from one of the staffed information desks or consult the interactive store finders.

o Dubai Mall is busiest on Thursday and Friday evenings.

o For close-ups of the Dubai Fountain show, board an abra (wooden ferry) that sets sail for 25-minute rides between 5.45pm and 11.30pm (Dhs65).

✕ Take a Break

Ice-cream fans will be in ecstasy over the creamy flavours of **Morelli's Gelato** (☎ 04 339 9053; www.morellisgelato.com; lower ground fl, Dubai Mall; per scoop Dhs19; ⏱10am-midnight; P📶; Ⓜ Burj Khalifa/Dubai Mall).

Sample modern Emirati cuisine at **Milas** (☎ 04 388 2313; http://milas.cc; ground fl, The Village, Dubai Mall, Sheikh Mohammed bin Rashid Blvd; mains Dhs48-95; ⏱9am-midnight Sun-Wed, to 1am Thu-Sat; P📶; Ⓜ Burj Khalifa/Dubai Mall).

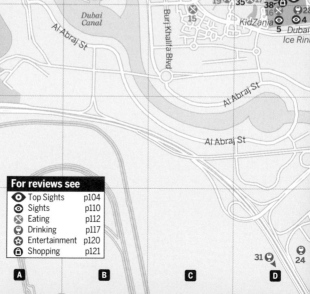

A B C D

1

Umm Amara St

13th St

Al Safa St

Sheikh Zayed
Rd Marine
Station

2
Sheikh Zayed
Bridge
Waterfall
6

58A

Burj
Khalifa/
Dubai Mall
M Interchange
No 1

Sheikh Zayed Rd

33

22

DOWNTOWN
DUBAI

Sheikh
Mohammed Bin
Rashid Blvd

Financial
Centre Rd

Al Saada St

Al Khaleej Al Tijari St

Al Saada St

3

Al Aamal St

23

37

Al Abraj St

32

Burj
Khalifa

29

Duba
Mall

12

18

9

36

39

19

35

17

38

16

28

Dubai Canal

15

KidZania

5

4

Burj Khalifa Blvd

Dubai
Ice Rink

Al Abraj St

4

Al Abraj St

Al Abraj St

5

For reviews see

⊙	Top Sights	p104
⊙	Sights	p110
⊗	Eating	p112
⊜	Drinking	p117
✪	Entertainment	p120
⊡	Shopping	p121

6

31

24

A B C D

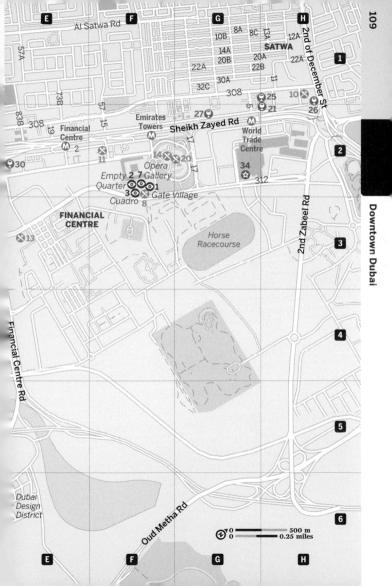

Downtown Dubai

E F G H

Al Satwa Rd

57A

10B 8A 8C 13A 12A
SATWA
14A
22A 20B 20A 22A
22B
32C 30A 11
73B 308
57 15
83B 308 25 10
19 21 26
Emirates 27 5
Financial Towers Sheikh Zayed Rd World
Centre Trade
2 M Centre
11 M 312
30 14 20 34
Opera 17
Empty 2 7 Gallery 17
Quarter 1
3 Gate Village
Cuadro 8

FINANCIAL
CENTRE

13

Horse
Racecourse

2nd December St

2nd Zabeel Rd

Financial Centre Rd

Dubai
Design
District

Oud Metha Rd

500 m
0.25 miles

1

2

3

4

5

6

Sights

Gate Village AREA

1 ◉ MAP P108, F2

Two wooden bridges link the massive Dubai International Finance Centre to Gate Village, a modernist cluster of 10 midrise stone-clad towers built around walkways and small piazzas. This is where many of Dubai's high-end Middle Eastern art galleries, including **Ayyam** (📞 04 439 2395; www.ayyamgallery. com; Bldg 3, Gate Village, DIFC; ⏱10am-10pm Sun-Wed, 2-10pm Thu & Sat) and Cuadro (p110), have set up shop, alongside posh eateries like Zuma (p112). Note that the place is all but dead on Fridays and Saturdays. (Happiness St; admission free; P; MEmirates Towers)

Empty Quarter GALLERY

2 ◉ MAP P108, F2

It's always worth stopping by this top-notch gallery, which is the only one in the UAE focused entirely on fine-art photography. While providing a platform for emerging talent, curators also put on shows featuring top international shutterbugs like Steve McCurry, Bruno Barbey, Marc Riboud and Al Moutasim Al Maskery. Many capture the zeitgeist with evocative, provocative or political themes.

It's part of the Gate Village gallery district at DIFC.

Cuadro GALLERY

3 ◉ MAP P108, F2

In a fabulous space taking up the entire ground floor of Gate Village's Building 10, this highly regarded gallery shines the spotlight on midcareer and established contemporary artists and sculptors, mostly from the Middle East. Some exhibits are based on work produced by artists participating in Cuadro's residency program. Lectures, workshops and panel discussions are also part of the gallery's schedule. (📞 04 425 0400; www.cuadroart.com; Bldg 10, Gate Village; ⏱10am-8pm Sun-Thu, noon-6pm Sat; MEmirates Towers)

Dubai Ice Rink ICE SKATING

4 ◉ MAP P108, D4

This Olympic-size ice rink inside Dubai Mall is ringed with cafes and restaurants and can even be converted into a concert arena. Sign up for a private or group class if you're a little wobbly in the knees. There are DJ sessions for families in the afternoons as well as nighttime disco sessions for shaking it up on the ice. (📞 04 437 1111; www. dubaiicerink.com; ground fl, Dubai Mall; per session incl skates Dhs60-100; ⏱10am-midnight; 👫; MBurj Khalifa/ Dubai Mall)

Sheik Zayed Bridge Waterfall

KidZania
AMUSEMENT PARK

5 ⊚ MAP P108, D4

For guilt-free shopping without your kids, drop them off in this indoor miniature city – complete with a school, a fire station, a hospital and a bank – where they get to dress up and slip into adult roles to playfully explore what it's like to be a fire-fighter, doctor, mechanic, pilot or other professional. (☎04 448 5222; www.kidzania.ae; 2nd fl, Dubai Mall; tickets from Dhs150; ⊘10am-11pm; P ⏸; M Burj Khalifa/Dubai Mall)

Sheikh Zayed Bridge Waterfall
WATERFALL

6 ⊚ MAP P108, A2

This illuminated and motion-operated waterfall cascades down both sides of Sheikh Zayed Bridge, stopping only for passing vessels. (Dubai Canal, Sheikh Zayed Bridge; admission free; ⊘7-10pm; M Business Bay)

Opera Gallery
GALLERY

7 ⊚ MAP P108, F2

More an art showroom than a classically curated gallery, Opera caters to collectors of artistic heavyweights in genres as varied as pop art, calligraphy and landscapes. One section of the striking bilevel space is reserved for contemporary artists from the Middle East.

Opera was founded in Paris in 1994; the Dubai branch is one of a dozen around the world. (☎04 323 0909; www.operagallery.com; Bldg 3, Gate Village; ⊘10am-10pm Sun-Wed, to midnight Thu, 2-9pm Fri, 11am-9pm Sat; M Emirates Towers)

Dubai Design District

The fresh-off-the-drawing board **Dubai Design District** (d3; Map p109, E6; ☑04 433 3000; www.dubaidesigndistrict.com; off Al Khail Rd, Business Bay; Ⓟ; 🚇Dubai Design District, ⓂBusiness Bay) has attracted both regional and international talent and brands, including hot shots like Adidas and Foster + Partners. Visitors can tap into this laboratory of tastemakers by checking out the edgy architecture and public art, browsing showrooms and pop-ups, eavesdropping on bearded hipsters in sleek cafes, or attending a free cultural event. It's 20 minutes by bus D03 or D03A from Dubai Mall/Burj Khalifa metro station.

Eating

Zuma
JAPANESE $$$

 8 MAP P108, F2

Every dish speaks of refinement in this perennially popular bilevel restaurant that gives classic Japanese fare an up-to-the-minute workout. No matter if you go for the top-cut sushi morsels (the dynamite spider roll is a serious eye-catcher!), meat and seafood tickled by the robata grill, or such signature dishes as miso-marinated black cod, you'll be keeping your taste buds happy. (☑04 425 5660; www.zumarestaurant.com; Bldg 06, Gate Village, Happiness St, DIFC; set lunches Dhs130, mains Dhs115-850; ⊙noon-3.30pm Sun-Thu, 12.30-4pm Fri, 12.30-4pm Sat & 7pm-midnight Sat-Wed, to 1am Thu & Fri; 🛜; ⓂEmirates Towers)

Baker & Spice
INTERNATIONAL $$

9 MAP P108, D3

A pioneer of the local-organic-fresh maxim in Dubai, this London import offers a seasonal bounty of dishes, prepared in-house and serves amid charming, country-style decor and on a Dubai Fountain–facing terrace. The salad bar brims with inspired creations, the breakfasts are tops and the meat and fish dishes sustainably sourced. (☑04 425 2240; www.bakerandspiceme.com; Souk Al Bahar; mains Dhs80-150; ⊙8am-11pm; 🛜🖉; ⓂBurj Khalifa/Dubai Mall)

Sum of Us
CAFE $$

10 MAP P108, H1

This two-floor industrial-style and plant-filled cafe with outdoor seating roasts its own beans, bakes its own sourdough bread and serves food that is at once comforting and exciting. All-day breakfast choices include French toast with salted caramel sauce, while the cauliflower risotto makes for an interesting main dish. (☑056 445 7526; www.thesumofusdubai.com; ground fl, Burj Al Salam Bldg, 6th St;

mains Dhs50-90; ⏱8am-midnight;
🅿🛜🗝; Ⓜ World Trade Centre)

Zaroob
LEBANESE $

11 ❌ MAP P108, F2

With its live cooking stations, open kitchens, fruit-filled baskets, colourful lanterns and graffiti-festooned steel shutters, Zaroob radiates the urban integrity of a Beirut street-food alley. Feast on such delicious no-fuss food as falafel (deep-fried chickpea balls), shawarma (spit-roasted meat in pita bread), flat or wrapped *manoushe* (Levant-style pizza) or *alayet* (tomato stew), all typical of the Levant. Nice terrace, too. (📞04 327 6262; www.zaroob.com; ground fl, Jumeirah Tower Building, Sheikh Zayed Rd; dishes Dhs12-32; ⏱24hr; 🅿🛜🗝; Ⓜ Emirates Towers, Financial Centre)

Leila
LEBANESE $$

12 ❌ MAP P108, C3

This Beirut import serves grannie-style rural Lebanese cafe cuisine adapted for the 21st century; light, healthy and fresh. The homey decor more than dabbles in the vintage department with its patterned wallpaper, crisp table cloths and floral dishes. It's also a nice spot for breakfast and *sheesha*. (📞04 448 3384; http://leilarestaurant.ae; Sheikh Mohammed bin Rashid Blvd; mains Dhs23-68; ⏱9.30am-12.45am Mon-Sat, to 1.45am Sat & Sun; 🛜; Ⓜ Burj Khalifa/Dubai Mall)

The Daily
BISTRO $$

13 ❌ MAP P108, E3

Warehouse-style decor, floor-to-ceiling windows and an outdoor terrace – overlooking Burj Khalifa, no less – make an instant impression at this casual all-day spot. Add in warm service and easygoing food (shakshuka eggs, superfood salads, steak and chips) at very reasonable prices, and you know you're onto a winner. Wash it down with fresh juices, barista-made coffee and well-priced beer and wine. (📞04 561 9999; www.rovehotels.com/the-daily; Rove Downtown, 312 Happiness St; mains Dhs45-120, brunch Dhs99; ⏱6.30am-11.30pm; Ⓜ Financial Centre, Burj Khalifa/Dubai Mall)

Al Nafoorah
LEBANESE $$$

14 ❌ MAP P108, F2

In this clubby, wood-panelled dining room the vast selection of delectable mezze is more impressive than the kebabs, but ultimately there are few false notes on the classic Lebanese menu. Even in summer you can sit on the terrace beneath an air-conditioned marquee. (📞04 432 3232; www.jumeirah.com; lower fl, Boulevard, Jumeirah Emirates Towers; mezze Dhs38-60, mains Dhs65-200; ⏱noon-3.30pm & 6-11.30pm; 🅿🛜🗝; Ⓜ Emirates Towers)

La Serre Bistro & Boulangerie
MEDITERRANEAN $$$

15 ❌ MAP P108, C4

Downtown residents regularly swing by the downstairs

Dining in Thin Air: At.mosphere

The food may not be out of this world, but the views are certainly stellar from the world's highest (442m) restaurant (www.atmosphere burjkhalifa.com) in the Burj Khalifa. Book far ahead to enjoy the views and international fare with an emphasis on seafood. The per-person minimum spend in the restaurant is Dhs500 at lunch and Dhs680 for dinner (Dhs880 for window table). If that's too dear, head one floor up to the lounge level where minimums are Dhs200 for breakfast, Dhs420 for afternoon tea and Dhs320 for dinner. No children under 10 are allowed. Dress nicely. The entrance is through the Armani Hotel.

boulangerie (bakery) for buttery croissants, toothsome pastries or petit déjeuner (breakfast) on the terrace, while gourmets on a spending spree head one floor up to tuck into minty prawn risotto, truffle-encrusted turbot and other fanciful dishes in the breezy dining room. (📞04 428 6969; www.laserre. ae; Vida Downtown Dubai, Sheikh Mohammed Bin Rashid Blvd; bistro mains Dhs120-230; ⏱bistro noon-3.15pm & 7-11pm, boulangerie 6.30am-10.30pm; P🛜✏️; MBurj Khalifa/ Dubai Mall)

Eataly
ITALIAN $$

16 🍴 MAP P108, D4

Italy's popular shop-cum-cafe has landed in Dubai Mall, bringing artisanal morsels from around the Boot to discerning palates. Stock up on pesto from Liguria, balsamico from Modena, olive oil from Sicily, and mozzarella and pasta made right in the store. Alternatively, stay and fill your stomach with pizza, panino or

pasta freshly prepared at several food stations.

For kids it's fun to watch the action and perhaps finish up the meal with a trip to the Nutella bar. (📞04 330 8899; www.eatalyarabia. com; lower ground fl, Dubai Mall; mains Dhs45-120; ⏱9am-11.30pm Sun-Wed, to 12.30am Thu-Sat; P🛜♿; MBurj Khalifa/Dubai Mall)

Karma Kafé
ASIAN $$$

17 🍴 MAP P108, D3

At this hip outpost a large Buddha guards the dining room dressed in sensuous burgundy with gold leaf accents. The menu hopscotches around Asia with classic and innovative sushi alongside such mains as tea-smoked salmon, Wagyu beef sliders from the robata grill, and black miso cod. The terrace has sublime Dubai Fountain views. (📞04 423 0909; www.karma-kafe. com; Souk Al Bahar; mains Dhs60-200; ⏱3pm-2am Sun-Thu, noon-2am Fri & Sat; 🛜; MBurj Khalifa/Dubai Mall)

Asado

ARGENTINE $$$

18 ⊗ MAP P108, C3

Meat lovers will be in heaven at this rustic-elegant lair with stellar views of the Burj Khalifa from the terrace tables. Start with a selection of stuffed *empanadas* (bread pockets) before treating yourself to a juicy grilled Argentine steak or the signature baby goat, slowly tickled to succulent perfection on an outdoor charcoal grill. Reservations essential. (☑04 428 7888; www.theaddress.com; ground fl, Palace Downtown, Mohammed bin Rashid Blvd; mains Dhs95-570; ☺6.30-11.30pm; P🛜; MBurj Khalifa/Dubai Mall)

Thiptara at Palace Downtown

THAI $$$

19 ⊗ MAP P108, C3

Thiptara means 'magic at the water' – very appropriate given its romantic setting in a lakeside pagoda with unimpeded views of the Dubai Fountain. The menu presents elegant interpretations of classic Thai dishes perked up by herbs grown by the chef himself. The green papaya salad, grilled black cod and green chicken curry are all solid menu picks. (☑04 428 7888; www.theaddress.com; Mohammed bin Rashid Blvd; mains Dhs120-290; ☺6-11.30pm; P🛜; MBurj Khalifa/Dubai Mall)

Eataly

Religion on a Plate

A Question of Pork

Muslims don't eat pork: it is haram, forbidden by Islam, as pigs are considered unclean. Alcohol is forbidden because it makes followers forgetful of God and prayer. The other major dietary restriction applies to meat: it must be halal, meaning religiously suitable or permitted. The animal must be drained of its blood at the time of slaughter by having its throat cut. That is why much of the red meat slaughtered and sold locally is very pale in colour. In restaurants, you will easily find nonhalal beef – just don't expect your tenderloin to be wrapped in a fatty strip of bacon before it's grilled.

Restaurants & Supermarkets

Some supermarkets sell beef and turkey bacon as an alternative to pork bacon, though hypermarkets such as Carrefour and Spinney's have dedicated 'pork rooms' that sell the real thing – they may not officially be entered by Muslims. To serve pork in a restaurant, you must have a pork licence. Likewise with alcohol, which is generally only served in hotels. If an item on a restaurant menu has been prepared with either alcohol or pork, it must be clearly marked.

Ramadan

The holy month of Ramadan is a time of spiritual contemplation for Muslims, who must fast from sunrise to sunset. Non-Muslim visitors are not expected to fast, but they should not smoke, drink or eat (including gum-chewing) in public during daylight hours. Business premises and hotels make provisions for the nonfasting by erecting screens around dining areas.

Ramadan would seem to be the ideal time to lose weight, yet lots of people pile on the pounds. The fast is broken each day with a communal breakfast comprising something light (such as dates and laban – an unsweetened yoghurt drink) before prayers. Then comes *iftar* at which enough food is usually consumed to compensate for the previous hours of abstinence with socialising that continues well into the early hours. With hundreds of restaurants putting on good-value *iftar* buffets, the temptation to overindulge is everywhere.

Noodle House   ASIAN $$

20 MAP 108, G2

This multibranch pan-Asian joint, where you order by ticking dishes on a tear-off menu pad, is a reliably good choice for a casual lunch or dinner. There's great variety – from roast duck to noodle soups to pad thai – and a spice-level indicator to please disparate tastes. (☑04 319 8088; www.thenoodlehouse.com; ground fl, Boulevard Mall, Emirates Towers, Sheikh Zayed Rd; mains Dhs35-90; ☺noon-midnight; P 🛜; M Emirates Towers)

Drinking

Cirque Le Soir   CLUB

21 MAP P108, H2

Is it a nightclub, a circus or a cabaret? One of Dubai's hottest after-dark spots – and London spin-off – is actually a trifecta of all three, a madhouse where you can let your freak out among clowns, stilt-walkers, sword swallowers and Dubai party A-listers. Musicwise it's mostly EDM, but hip-hop Mondays actually draw some of the biggest crowds. (☑050 995 5400; www.facebook.com/CirqueLeSoirDubai; Fairmont Hotel, Sheikh Zayed Rd; ☺10.30pm-3am Mon, Tue, Thu & Fri; M World Trade Centre)

Bridgewater Tavern   SPORTS BAR

22 🍺 MAP P108, A2

This happening joint has ushered the sports bar into a new era. Sure, there are the requisite big screens to catch the ball action, but it's packaged into an industrial-flavoured space with (mostly) rock on the turntables, *sheesha* on the canalside terrace, and an elevated gastropub menu whose signature 'black' burger is so messy it comes with a bib! (☑04 414 0000; www.jwmarriottmarquisdubailife.com/dining/bridgewatertavern; JW Marriott Marquis Hotel, Sheikh Zayed Rd; ☺4pm-2am; 🛜; M Business Bay)

Treehouse   BAR

23 🍺 MAP P108, C3

At the top of the Taj, this luxe lair treats guests to unimpeded views of the Burj Khalifa, top-shelf drinks and an outdoor living room setting with potted plants, pillow-packed sofas, pink marble tables and even a candlelit mock fireplace. A chill spot for quiet conversation on weekdays, the action picks up with deep-house DJs on weekends. (☑04 438 3100; www.treehousedubai.com; Taj Dubai Hotel, Burk Khalifa Blvd; ☺6pm-1am Sat-Wed, to 2am Thu & Fri; M Business Bay)

Base   CLUB

24 🍺 MAP P108, D6

This b-i-g next-gen nightclub holds forth under open skies in the Dubai Design District and can host up 5000 people for concerts and parties. Expect a top-notch sound system, a top line-up, pyrotechnics and shiny happy people. (☑055 313 4999; www.basedubai.com; Dubai Design District; ☺10.30-3am Sep-May; M Business Bay)

Burj Khalifa: Facts & Figures

The Burj Khalifa is not only the world's tallest building (for now) but also flaunts other records and impressive figures:

- tallest free-standing structure highest outdoor observation deck (555m)
- highest occupied floor (160th fl, at 585.5m) longest elevator (504m)
- highest number of floors (211)
- highest restaurant (122nd fl, 452m)
- weight of concrete use is equivalent to 100,000 elephants
- the service elevator has a carrying capacity of 5500kg
- the facade is made of 28,261 glass panels
- it takes three to four months to clean the facade
- in 2011, French climber Alain Robert scaled the Burj in just over six hours
- in 2014 two other Frenchmen (Vincent Reffet and Frédéric Fugen) set the world record base jump from the Burj

Cavalli Club   CLUB

25 🚇 MAP P108, H1

Black limos jostle for position outside this over-the-top lair where you can sip Robert Cavalli vodka-based cocktails and dine on Italian fare served on Cavalli plates with Cavalli cutlery amid a virtual Aladdin's cave of black quartz and Swarovski crystals. Ladies, wear those vertiginous heels or risk feeling frumpy. Men, dress snappy or forget about it. The entrance is behind the hotel. (📞050 991 0400; http://dubai.cavalliclub.com; Fairmont Hotel, Sheikh Zayed Rd; ⏲8.30pm-3am; 🛜; Ⓜ World Trade Centre)

40 Kong   BAR

26 🚇 MAP P108, H1

Finance moguls and corporate execs mix it up at this intimate rooftop cocktail bar perched atop the 40th floor of the H Hotel with views of the World Trade Centre and Sheikh Zayed Rd. The twin-kling lanterns and palm trees set romantic accents for post-work or post-shopping sundowners, paired with global bar bites. (📞04 355 8896; www.40kong.com; 40th fl, H Hotel, Sheikh Zayed Rd; ⏲7pm-3am; 🛜; Ⓜ World Trade Centre)

Fibber Magee's   PUB

27 🚇 MAP P109, G2

Been-around-forever Fibbers is an amiably scruffy morning to night pub with Guinness and Kilkenny on tap, all-day breakfast plus a menu of international comfort food designed to keep brains in balance, and sports (rugby to horse racing) on the big screens. Traditional Irish music on Thursday nights puts a tear in many expat eyes. (☑04 332 2400; www.fibbersdubai.com; Saeed Tower One, Sheikh Zayed Rd; ☺8am-2am; 🛜; Ⓜ World Trade Centre)

Majlis
CAFE

28 🔲 MAP P108, D4

If you ever wanted to find out how to milk a camel (and who doesn't?), watch the video on the interactive iPad menu of this pretty cafe while sipping a camelccino (camel-milk cappuccino) or date-flavoured camel milk. Nibbles, desserts, chocolate and cheese, all

made with camel milk, beckon as well. (☑056 287 1522; ground fl, Gold Souk, Dubai Mall; ☺10am-midnight; 🛜; Ⓜ Burj Khalifa/Dubai Mall)

Cabana
BAR, LOUNGE

29 🔲 MAP P108, D3

A laid-back poolside vibe combines with urban sophistication and stellar views of the Burj Khalifa at this alfresco restaurant and terrace lounge. A DJ plays smooth tunes that don't hamper animated conversation. Cap off a Dubai Mall shopping spree at a happy hour which runs from 2pm to 8pm. (☑04 438 8888; www.theaddress. com; 3rd fl, Address Dubai Mall Hotel, Sheikh Mohammed bin Rashid Blvd; ☺8.30am-12am; 🛜; Ⓜ Burj Khalifa/Dubai Mall)

40 Kong

Nippon Bottle Company   BAR

30 🕐 MAP P108, E2

Finding this neon-lit Japanese bar, hidden speakeasy-style behind a bookcase off the lobby of the Dusit Thani Hotel, requires a clear head, which you may no longer have after sampling its potent cocktails and Japanese whiskeys. (www.dusit.com/dusitthani/dubai; Dusit Thani Hotel, Sheikh Zayed Rd; ⊙6pm-3am; Ⓜ Financial Centre)

White Dubai   CLUB

31 🕐 MAP P108, D6

The Dubai spawn of the Beirut original did not need long to lure local socialites with high-energy rooftop parties under the stars. International spinmeisters shower party-goers with an eclectic sound soup, from house and electro to bump-and-grind hip-hop and R & B, all fuelled by dazzling projections and light shows.

It's the only Middle Eastern club on *DJ Mag*'s Top 100 list. (📞050 443 0933; www.whitedubai.com; Meydan Racecourse Grandstand Rooftop, Nad Al Sheba; ⊙11pm-3am Tue, Thu-Sat)

Entertainment

Dubai Opera   PERFORMING ARTS

32 ⭐ MAP P108, C3

Shaped like a traditional dhow – the sailing vessels that still ply the Gulf – Dubai Opera is the city's newest high-calibre performing-arts venue. Despite its name, it actually hosts a wide range of shows, including musicals, ballet, comedy acts, rock bands and recitals. The 'bow' of the building contains a 2000-seat theatre and glass-fronted foyer overlooking Burj Lake. (📞04 440 8888; www.dubaiopera.com; Sheikh Mohammed Bin Rashid Blvd; Ⓜ Burj Khalifa/Dubai Mall)

La Perle by Dragone   PERFORMING ARTS

33 ⭐ MAP P108, A2

A custom-designed theatre with a 270-degree angle make for perfect sight lines even in the cheaper seats of this magical show centred on a aquatic stage where some 65 acrobats perform their stunning stunts. It is the brainchild of Franco Dragone, one of the original creators of Cirque du Soleil. (https://laperle.com; Al Habtorr City; tickets Dhs400-1600; 🛜; Ⓜ Business Bay)

Blue Bar   LIVE MUSIC

34 ⭐ MAP P108, G2

Cool cats of all ages gather in this relaxed joint for some of the finest live jazz and blues in town along with a full, reasonably priced bar lineup that includes signature cocktails named after jazz greats (try the Louis Armstrong–inspired Hello Dolly). It's open daily with live concerts from 10pm Thursday to Saturday. (📞04 310 8150; www.facebook.com/BlueBarNovotelWTC; Novotel World Trade Centre Dubai, Happiness St; ⊙noon-2am; 🛜; Ⓜ World Trade Centre)

Shopping

Souk Al Bahar   MALL

35 🔒 MAP P108, D3

Translated as 'market of the sailor', Souk Al Bahar is a small arabesque-style mall next to the Dubai Mall that sells mostly tourist-geared items. It's really more noteworthy for its enchanting design (arch-lined stone corridors, dim lighting) and Dubai Fountain–facing restaurants, some of which are licensed. Also handy: a branch of Spinneys supermarket in the basement. (www.soukalbahar. ae; Old Town Island; ⏰10am-10pm Sun-Thu, 2-10pm Fri; 📶; Ⓜ Burj Khalifa/Dubai Mall)

Kinokuniya   BOOKS

36 🔒 MAP P108, D3

This massive store is El Dorado for bookworms. Shelves are stocked with a mind-boggling half-a-million tomes plus 1000 or so magazines in English, Arabic, Japanese, French, German and Chinese. (📞04 434 0111; www.kinokuniya.com/ ae; 2nd fl, Dubai Mall; ⏰10am-midnight; 📶; Ⓜ Burj Khalifa/Dubai Mall)

Farmers Market on the Terrace   MARKET

37 🔒 MAP P108, C3

The carrots may have roots attached and dirt might stick to the fennel bulb, because both were still in the ground the previous day. Now they're vying for customers at this small farmers market, which brings organic, locally grown produce straight from grower to grazer. (📞04 427 9856; www.face book.com/TheFarmersMarketOnThe Terrace; Bay Avenue Park, Burj Khalifa & Al A'amal Sts, Business Bay; ⏰8am-1pm Fri Nov-May; Ⓜ Business Bay)

Candylicious   FOOD

38 🔒 MAP P108, D3

Stand under the lollipop tree, watch the candymakers at work or gorge yourself on gourmet popcorn at this colourful candy emporium stocked to the rafters with everything from jelly beans to halal sweets and gourmet chocolate. Sweet bliss. Just don't tell your dentist. (📞04 330 8700; www. candyliciousshop.com; ground fl, Dubai Mall; ⏰10am-midnight; 📶; Ⓜ Burj Khalifa/Dubai Mall)

Nayomi   CLOTHING

39 🔒 MAP P108, D3

One of Dubai's raciest stores stocks push-up bras, high-heeled feathery slippers, slinky night gowns, seductive beauty products (we like the 'Booty Parlor' line) and other nocturnal niceties from – surprise! – Saudi Arabia. In fact, Nayomi, which means 'soft' and 'delicate' in Arabic, is a major brand all over the Middle East, with 10 branches around Dubai alone. (📞04 339 8820; www.nayomi.com; 1st fl, Dubai Mall; ⏰10am-10pm Sun-Wed, to midnight Thu-Sat; 📶; Ⓜ Burj Khalifa/Dubai Mall)

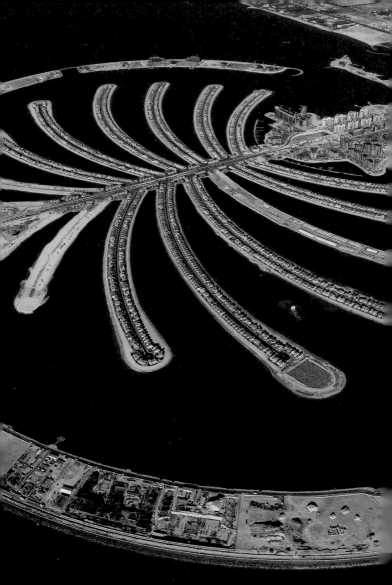

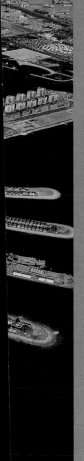

Explore

Dubai Marina & Palm Jumeirah

These popular upscale residential areas are lined with luxurious beachfront resorts. Other diversions here include strolls along the Dubai Marina waterfront, The Walk at JBR and The Beach at JBR, and – soon – rides on the world's largest observation wheel.

Carved from the desert, Dubai Marina is one of the world's largest artificial marinas, centred on a 3km-long canal flanked by a thicket of futuristic high-rises. After dusk when you can gaze out at the glittering towers and bobbing yachts, stop by the dancing fountains and find your favourite dinner, drink or sheesha spot.

Paralleling the beach are The Walk at JBR, a 1.7km-long strip of shops and eateries, and The Beach at JBR, a chic open-air mall fronting a lovely sandy beach with great infrastructure. Just offshore is Bluewaters Islands, where the world's largest observation wheel, Ain Dubai, will soon start making its merry rounds. The Dubai Tram threads through much of the Marina.

Jutting into the Gulf is the Palm Jumeirah, an artificial island in the shape of a palm tree with a 2km-long trunk, 16-frond crown and 11km-long crescent-shaped breakwater.

Getting There & Around

Ⓜ **Damac** (for Dubai Marina) / **Jumeirah Lakes Towers** (for The Beach at JBR and The Walk at JBR)

🚋 Links Dubai Media City, JBR and Dubai Marina on an 11km loop.

Dubai Marina & Palm Jumeirah Map on p126

Palm Jumeirah YANN ARTHUS-BERTRAND/GETTY IMAGES ©

Walking Tour 🚶

Dubai Marina Walk

Built around a 3km-long canal flanked by a thicket of futuristic high-rises, the Dubai Marina is one of the world's largest marinas. A saunter along its promenade is delightful, especially after dusk, when you can gaze out at the glittering towers and yachts, stop by the dancing fountains and stake out your favourite dinner, drink or sheesha spot.

Walk Facts

Start Cayan Tower

End Barracuda

Length 2.5km; as long as you like

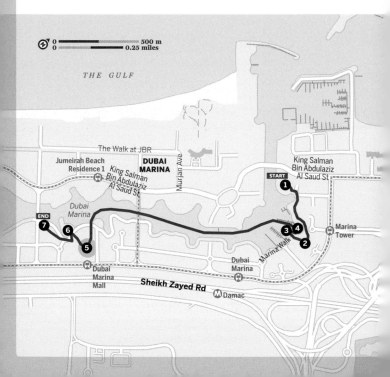

❶ Cayan Tower

This architectural **stunner** (Al Sharta St; Ⓜ Damac, 🚇 Marina Towers) is quite literally a building with a twist as its 75 stories spiral over 307m at a 90-degree angle. Designed by Skidmore, Owings & Merrill (SOM), which also masterminded the Burj Khalifa, it is the most eye-catching in the phalanx of high-rises in the Dubai Marina.

❷ Bicycle Cruising

Nextbike (Byky; www.nextbike. net; 1/2/5/24hr Dhs20/25/40/80; ⏱24hr) lets you pick up and drop off bicycles at numerous stations dotted around the Dubai Marina and Palm Jumeirah, including one next to Spinneys supermarket. All you need to do is register first via its website, which also has full details about how the scheme works.

❸ Sheesha Chilling

Reem al Bawadi (www.reemalbawa di.com; Marina Walk; sheesha Dhs50; ⏱9am-3am; Ⓜ Damac) has several outlets across town, but this one has the nicest ambience. Kick back on the terrace or report to the cosy interior with its complexion-friendly lamps and ample arches, nooks and crannies. A full menu of mezze and sheesha is served.

❹ Water Bus

For a scenic spin around the marina, hop on the **Water Bus** (www.rta.ae; tickets Dhs3-11, one-day pass Dhs25; ⏱10am-11pm Sat-Thu,

noon-midnight Fri; Ⓜ Damac), which shuttles between the Marina Walk, Marina Terrace, Marina Mall and the Promenade every 15 minutes. It's lovely at sunset or after dark when you float past the show-stopping parade of shimmering towers.

❺ Dubai Marina Mall

With only 140 stores, **Dubai Marina Mall** (p139) may not rank among the city's megamalls, yet the shops are just as good and you won't get lost so readily. Its main architectural feature is the giant atrium where kids can trundle around in a toy train.

❻ Gourmet Tower

The seven-storey **Pier 7** (p130) is a feast for foodies, with each floor holding a hip restaurant or bar with terraces delivering stunning views of bobbing yachts and twinkling towers.Options include gourmet comfort food at Fümé, sizzling Asian at Asia Asia and rooftop cocktails at Atelier M.

❼ Seafood Feast

Empty tables are rare at **Barracuda** (📞 04 452 2278; www.facebook. com/barracudarestaurantuae; Silverene Tower, Marina Walk; mains Dhs50-215; ⏱noon-1am; 📶; Ⓜ Jumeirah Lakes Tower, 🚇 Dubai Marina Mall), an Egyptian seafood shrine where the catch of the day is theatrically displayed on ice. Have it oven-grilled or simply drizzled with olive oil and lemon.

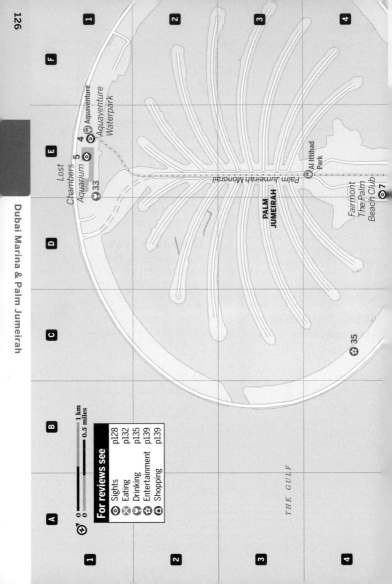

Dubai Marina & Palm Jumeirah

For reviews see

⊙ Sights	p128
⊗ Eating	p132
❶ Drinking	p135
✪ Entertainment	p139
⊟ Shopping	p139

0 ___ 1 km
0 ___ 0.5 miles

THE GULF

Lost Chambers Aquarium ⊙ 5

🏛 Aquaventure

⊙ 4 Aquaventure Waterpark

⊗ 33

Palm Jumeirah Monorail

PALM JUMEIRAH

Al Ittihad Park

Fairmont The Palm Beach Club

❶ 7

✪ 35

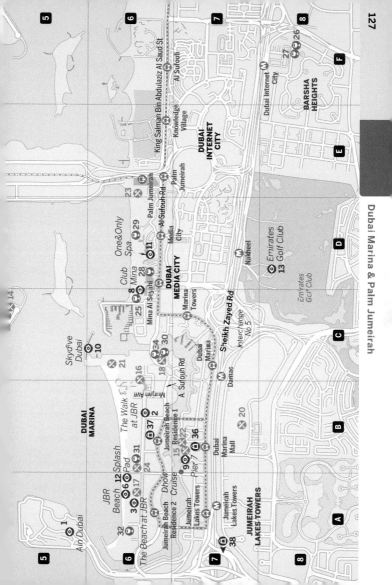

Dubai Marina & Palm Jumeirah

Sights

Ain Dubai

FERRIS WHEEL

1 ◎ MAP P126, A5

Opening in 2018, Dubai will be able to lay claim to to yet another record: the world's tallest observation wheel. Ain Dubai will rise 210m on artificial Bluewaters Island off the coast of Jumeirah Beach Residence, making it 43m higher than current record-holder, the High Roller in Las Vegas. Up to 1400 passengers get to enjoy 360-degree views of the Dubai skyline during the 48-minute rotation, seated in 48 enclosed cabins outfitted with stone floors and benches. (✆800 637 227; www. bluewatersdubai.ae; Bluewaters Island, Dubai Marina; Ⓜ Jumeirah Lakes Towers, 🚊 Jumeirah Beach Residence 2)

The Walk at JBR

AREA

2 ◎ MAP P126, B6

In a city of air-conditioned malls, this attractive outdoor shopping and dining promenade was an immediate hit when it opened in 2008. Join locals and expats in strolling the 1.7km stretch, watching the world on parade from a pavement cafe, browsing the fashionable boutiques or ogling the shiny Ferraris and other fancy cars cruising by on weekends. (Jumeirah Beach Residence, Dubai Marina; Ⓜ Jumeirah Lakes Towers, Damac, 🚊 Jumeirah Beach Residence 1, Jumeirah Beach Residence 2)

The Beach at JBR

AREA

3 ◎ MAP P126, A6

Paralleling the beachfront for about 1km, The Beach is an open-plan cluster of low-lying, urban-style buildings wrapped around breezy plazas. Hugely popular with families on weekends, it mixes cafes and upmarket shops with a lively waterfront fun zone complete with a kiddie splash park, an outdoor gym, a crafts market and other diversions. A beach club rents sunloungers, but you're free to spread your towel just about anywhere for free. (✆04 317 3999; www.thebeach.ae; Jumeirah Beach Residence, Dubai Marina; admission free; ⏲10am-midnight Sun-Wed, to 1am Thu-Sat; P 🚻; Ⓜ Jumeirah Lakes Towers, Damac, 🚊Jumeirah Beach Residence 1, Jumeirah Beach Residence 2)

Aquaventure Waterpark

WATER PARK

4 ◎ MAP P126, E1

Adrenalin rushes are guaranteed at this water park at Atlantis The Palm resort. A 1.6km-long 'river' with rapids, wave surges and waterfalls meanders through vast grounds that are anchored by two towers. A highlight is the ziggurat-shaped Tower of Neptune, with three slides, including the aptly named Leap of Faith, a near-vertical plunge into a shark-infested lagoon. (✆04 426 1169; www.atlantisthepalm.com; Atlantis The Palm, Palm Jumeirah; over/under 120cm tall Dhs260/215; ⏲10am-sunset; 🚻; 🚊Aquaventure)

Lost Chambers Aquarium

AQUARIUM

5 🎯 MAP P126, E1

Rare albino alligators Ali and Blue are the latest stars in this fantastic labyrinth of underwater halls, enclosures and fish tanks that re-creates the legend of the lost city of Atlantis. Some 65,000 exotic marine creatures inhabit 21 aquariums, where rays flutter, jellyfish dance and giant groupers lurk. The centrepiece is the Ambassador Lagoon. For an extra fee, you can snorkel or dive with the fishes in this 11.5-million-litre tank. (📞04 426 1040; www.atlantisthepalm.com; Atlantis The Palm, Palm Jumeirah; adult/child 3-11yr Dhs100/70; 🕙10am-10pm; 🅿; 🚊Aquaventure)

JBR Beach

BEACH

6 🎯 MAP P126, A6

This clean, wonderful playground has plenty of facilities, including showers, toilets and changing rooms housed in distinctive panelled pods. Kids can keep cool in a splash zone, and there's even an outdoor gym for pumping, Since it's right next to The Beach at JBR (p128) and The Walk at JBR (p128), there's no shortage of food and drink outlets, although alcohol is only available in the hotels. (Jumeirah Beach Residence, Dubai Marina; admission free; 👶; Ⓜ Jumeirah Lakes Towers, 🚊Jumeirah Lakes Towers)

The Walk at JBR

Fairmont The Palm Beach Club

BEACH

7 MAP P126, E4

Views back at the mainland skyline are one of the most memorable aspects of a day at this family-oriented club at the swish Fairmont Hotel. Parents get to wriggle their toes in the sand or by the pool while the little ones let off steam in the Fairmont Falcon Juniors' Club. (☏04 457 3388; www.fairmont.com/palm-dubai; Fairmont The Palm, Palm Jumeirah; day pass weekday/weekend adult Dhs250/300, child Dhs150; ☺6.30am-8pm; P⛱; MNakheel)

Club Mina

BEACH

8 MAP P126, C6

Set along 500m of private beach, this club is a family favourite thanks to its five pools (including a shaded one for kids), a kids' club and a water-sports centre. Nice touch for grown-ups: cocktails in the swim-up bar. (☏04 399 3333; www.clubminadubai.com; Le Meridien Mina Seyahi Beach Resort, King Salman Bin Abdul Aziz Al Saud St, Dubai Media City; day pass weekday/weekend adult Dhs225/350, child Dhs125/175; P⛱; MNahkeel)

Pier 7

NOTABLE BUILDING

9 MAP P126, B7

Linked to the Dubai Marina Mall via a glass-encased walkway, this circular tower gets its name from the seven restaurants – from Asian to French – on each of its floors. All but the lowest one have terrace tables for noshing with a view. (☏04 436 1020; www.pier7.ae; Marina Walk, Dubai Marina; MDamac, ⛟Dubai Marina Mall)

Skydive Dubai

SKYDIVING

10 MAP P126, C6

Daredevils can experience the rush of jumping out of a plane and seeing Palm Jumeirah and the

Desert Explorations

For travellers on short trips to Dubai, an organised 4WD desert safari is the most popular way to experience the Arabian sands. Typical tours involve off-roading, camel riding, henna painting and belly dancing, followed by a Middle Eastern dinner. Cheaper tours head for Al Awir, 35km east of Downtown, while a few companies, including **Platinum Heritage Tours** (☏04 388 4044; www.platinum-heritage.com; 3rd fl, Oasis Centre, Sheikh Zayed Rd, Al Quoz 1; ☺office hours 8am-6pm; MNoor Bank) and **Arabian Adventures** (☏800 272 2426, 04 303 4888; www.arabian-adventures.com; Sheikh Zayed Rd, Emirates Holiday Bldg), are permitted to take travellers into the Dubai Desert Conservation. Reserve for a more genuine, sustainable experience.

Dubai skyline from the air by signing up for these tandem parachute flights. The minimum age is 18; weight and height restrictions apply as well. (📞04 377 8888; www.skydivedubai.ae; Al Seyahi St, Dubai Marina; tandem jump, video & photos Dhs2000; ⏱8am-4pm Mon-Sat; Ⓜ Damac)

One&Only Spa
SPA

11 ⊙ MAP P126, D6

Do you want to unwind, restore or elevate? These are the magic words at this exclusive spa with a dozen treatment rooms where massages, wraps, scrubs and facials are calibrated to achieve your chosen goal. Staff can help find the perfect massage or wrap for whatever ails you. A favourite is a session in the Oriental Hammam. (📞04 315 2140; http://royalmirage.oneandonlyresorts.com; One&Only Royal Mirage, King Salman Bin Abdul Aziz Al Saud St, Dubai Media City; ⏱9.30am-9pm (women only until 1pm); Ⓜ Nakheel)

Splash Pad
WATER PARK

12 ⊙ MAP P126, A6

Preschoolers can keep cool in the fountains, sprinklers, tipping buckets and other watery fun spots at this cheerfully coloured mini water park right next to the sand. The fenced-in area also includes a dry-play area with swings, see-saws and climbing frames. (www.splashpaddubai.com; The Beach at JBR, Dubai Marina; per 1/24hr Dhs65/95; ⏱9am-

Nostalgic Cruising

Local company **Tour Dubai** (Map p126, B7; 📞04 336 8407; www.tour-dubai.com; Tour Dubai, Marina Walk, below Al Gharbi St bridge, Dubai Marina; 1hr tour adult/child Dhs65/55, dinner cruises Dhs300/150; Ⓜ Jumeirah Lakes Towers, 🚊Dubai Marina Mall) runs guided one-hour boat tours with prerecorded English commentary aboard nostalgic dhows outfitted with colourful upholstered benches. There are eight tours daily between 10.30am and 5.30pm. In the evening, the dhows set sail for a two-hour dinner buffet with taped music. Alcohol is available.

8pm; 👫; Ⓜ Jumeirah Lakes Towers, 🚊Jumeirah Beach Residence 2)

Emirates Golf Club
GOLF

13 ⊙ MAP P126, D8

This prestigious club has two courses: the flagship international championship Majlis course, which hosts the annual **Dubai Desert Classic** (📞04 383 3588; www.omegadubaidesertclassic.com; Emirates Golf Club, Emirates Hills 2; tickets Dhs75-175; ⏱Feb; 🛜; Ⓜ Nakheel), and the Faldo course, which is the only floodlit 18-hole course in the country. Beginners can go wild on the par-three nine-hole course (peak/off-peak Dhs130/95).

Rates drop significantly from late May to mid-September. (📞04 380 1234, 04 417 9800; www.dubaigolf.com; Interchange No 5, Sheikh Zayed Rd, Emirates Hills 2; Majlis/Faldo Sun-Thu Dhs995/595, Fri & Sat Dhs1200/695; MNakheel)

Eating

Stay
FRENCH $$$

14 ❌ MAP P126, C5

Three-Michelin-starred Yannick Alléno brings his culinary magic to Dubai in this subtly theatrical vaulted dining room accented with black crystal chandeliers. His creations seem deceptively simple (the beef tenderloin with fries and blackpepper sauce is a bestseller), letting the superb ingredients shine brightly. An unexpected

stunner is the Pastry Library, an entire wall of sweet treats. (📞04 440 1030; http://thepalm.oneandonly resorts.com; One&Only The Palm, West Crescent, Palm Jumeirah; mains Dhs190-290; ⏰7-11pm Tue-Sun; P🛜; MNakheel, Dubai Internet City, Palm Atlantis)

Asia Asia
FUSION $$$

15 ❌ MAP P126, B7

Prepare for a culinary journey along the Spice Road at this theatrically decorated restaurant entered via a candlelit corridor that spills into an exotic booth-lined lounge with dangling birdcage lamps. Dim sum to tuna tataki and crispy duck – dishes here are alive with flavours from Asia and the Middle East. Bonus: the grand marina views from the terrace. Full

Mezze (selection of hot and cold dishes)

Ramadan

Ramadan falls into the ninth month of the Muslim calendar. It is considered a time of spiritual reflection and involves fasting during daylight hours.

Non-Muslims are not expected to follow suit, but visitors should not smoke, drink or eat (including chewing gum) in public during Ramadan. Hotels make provisions for non-Muslim guests by erecting screens for discreet dining. Opening hours tend to become shorter and more erratic. In 2016, Dubai relaxed restrictions on the daytime sale of alcohol in licensed bars. Some nightclubs are open as well, although live music is a no-no.

Once the sun has set, the fast is broken with something light before prayers. Then comes *iftar*, a big communal meal that non-Muslims are welcome to join in. Many restaurants and hotels set up big festive *iftar* tents. People then rise again before dawn to prepare a meal *(suhoor)* to support them through the day.

bar. (☑04 276 5900; www.asia-asia. com; 6th fl, Pier 7, Dubai Marina; mains Dhs90-350, ⏰4pm-midnight or later; 🛜; Ⓜ Damac, 🚃 Dubai Marina Mall)

Maya Modern Mexican Kitchen
MEXICAN $$$

16 ✗ MAP P126, C6

Richard Sandoval, the man who introduced modern Mexican food to the US, is behind the menu at this casual-chic restaurant. Expect a piñata of flavours, from creamy guacamole (prepared tableside of course) to fish tacos with peanut sauce, chicken *mole poblano* to sizzling prawn fajitas. Tip: get there before sunset for top-shelf margaritas on the rooftop lounge. Great brunch, too. (☑04 316 5550; www.maya-dubai.com; Le Royal Meridien Beach Resort & Spa, Al Mamsha

St, Dubai Marina; mains Dhs110-200, brunch without/with alcohol Dhs325/435; ⏰7pm-1am Mon-Sat; 🅿 🛜; Ⓜ Damac, 🚃 Jumeirah Beach Residence 1)

Bouchon Bakery
BAKERY $

17 ✗ MAP P126, A6

This classy cafe – an outpost of celebrity chef Thomas Keller's popular US chain – serves fiendishly good pastries, cakes and macrons. Everything is baked fresh each morning in the glass-walled kitchen, with a well-priced selection of soups, salads and sandwiches and excellent coffee. Grab a table on the terrace or slide into a dark-leather booth indoors to escape the sun. (☑04 419 0772; www.thebeach.ae; The Beach at JBR; pastries Dhs13-20, cakes Dhs20-24, mains Dhs50; ⏰8am-11pm Sun-Thu,

to midnight Fri & Sat; 🛜 📝;
Ⓜ Jumeirah Lakes Towers)

Indego by Vineet

INDIAN $$$

18 ❌ MAP P126, C6

India's first Michelin-starred chef, Vineet Bhatia, is the menu maven at this gorgeous, intimate dining room lorded over by big brass Natraj sculptures. Dishes straddle the line between tradition and innovation, usually with exciting results. (📞 04 317 6000; www.indego byvineet.com; ground fl, Tower One, Grosvenor House, Al Emreef St, Dubai Marina; mains Dhs115-240, brunch with/without alcohol Dhs350/250; 🕐 7pm-midnight; Ⓟ 🛜; Ⓜ Damac, 🚉 Jumeirah Beach Residence 1)

101 Lounge & Bar

MEDITERRANEAN $$$

19 ❌ MAP P126, C5

It may be hard to concentrate on the food at this marina-adjacent al fresco pavilion, with to-die-for views of the Dubai Marina skyline. Come for nibbles and cocktails in the bar or go for the full dinner experience (paella, grills, pastas). New: the ultraswish Champagne Bar. Ask about the free boat shuttle when making reservations. (📞 04 440 1010; http://thepalm. oneandonlyresorts.com; One&Only The Palm, West Crescent, Palm Jumeirah; mains Dhs85-295, tapas Dhs35-80; 🕐 11.30am-2am Mon-Sat; 🛜; Ⓜ Nakheel, Dubai Internet City, Atlantis Aquaventure)

Mythos Kouzina & Grill

GREEK $$

20 ❌ MAP P126, B7

Kitted out like a traditional seaside taverna with whitewashed walls and rustic furniture, Mythos is a little slice of Santorini hidden away in the somewhat incongruous setting of JLT's Armada BlueBay Hotel. Order a selection of starters to share – the *keftedakia* (meatballs) are particularly good – then it's a toss-up between home-style favourites like moussaka and souvlaki and succulent grilled meat and seafood. (📞 04 399 8166; www.mythoskouzina.com; Level B1, Armada BlueBay Hotel, Cluster P, Jumeirah Lakes Towers; mains Dhs45-89; 🕐 12:30-5pm & 7-11:30pm; Ⓜ Damac Properties)

Zero Gravity

INTERNATIONAL $$

21 ❌ MAP P126, C6

Next to the Skydive Dubai drop zone, this stylish outpost with attached beach club checks off all the culinary boxes, from breakfast to late-night snacks. Pizza, pasta, sandwiches, grills and salads are all fresh, healthy and perfectly pitched to mainstream tastes. (📞 04 399 0009; www.0-gravity. ae; Al Seyahi St, Skydive Dubai Drop Zone, Dubai Marina; mains Dhs50-250; 🕐 8am-2am; Ⓟ 🛜; Ⓜ Damac)

Fümé

INTERNATIONAL $$

22 ❌ MAP P126, B7

With its industrial-chic look, relaxed crew and global comfort

Dubai Tram

The Dubai Marina is one of the most pedestrian-friendly areas in town and is also served by the Dubai Tram (www.alsufouhtram. com), which makes 11 stops, including one near the Marina Mall, The Beach at JBR and The Walk at JBR. It also connects with the Damac and Jumeirah Lakes Towers metro stations and with the Palm Jumeirah Monorail at Palm Jumeirah station. Nol Cards (p148) must be used.

food, Fümé brings more than a touch of urban cool to the Marina. The menu features plenty of creative dishes to keep foodies happy, including the bestseller: super-juicy beef chuck ribs smoked for six hours in a closed charcoal oven. No reservations. (☏04 421 5669; www.fume-eatery.com; level 1, Pier 7, Marina Walk, Dubai Marina; mains Dhs55-125; ☺noon-2am Sat-Wed, 9am-2am Thu & Fri; ☎; Ⓜ Jumeirah Lakes Towers, ☖Dubai Marina Mall)

Eauzone ASIAN $$$

23 ✖ MAP P126, E6

This jewel of a restaurant draws friends, romancing couples and fashionable families to a sublime seaside setting with shaded wooden decks and floating *majlis* overlooking illuminated pools. Casual by day, it's hushed and intimate at night, perfect for concentrating on such pleasurable classics as lotus-wrapped sea bass or miso-glazed black cod. (☏04 399 9999; http://royalmirage.oneandonlyresorts.com; Arabian Court, One&Only Royal Mirage, King Salman Bin Abdul Aziz Al Saud St, Dubai Media City; mains Dhs80-165;

☺noon-3.30pm & 7-11.30pm; Ⓟ☎; Ⓜ Nakheel, ☖Palm Jumeirah)

BiCE ITALIAN $$$

24 ✖ MAP P126, B6

Back in 1930s Milan, Beatrice 'Bice' Ruggeri first opened her trattoria, which evolved into the city's most fashionable by the 1970s. Today, Dubai's BiCE carries on the tradition by adding creative touches to such classics as oven-baked sea bass and veal tenderloin with foie gras sauce. Nice touch: the olive-oil trolley. (☏04 399 1111; Hilton Dubai Jumeirah, The Walk at JBR, Dubai Marina; pasta Dhs70-195, mains Dhs150-230; ☺12.30-3.30pm & 7-11.30pm; Ⓟ☎; Ⓜ Jumeirah Lakes Towers, ☖Jumeirah Beach Residence 1, Jumeirah Beach Residence 2)

Drinking

Barasti BAR

25 🍺 MAP P126, C6

Since 1995, Barasti has grown from basic beach shack to top spot for lazy days in the sand and is often jam-packed with shiny

HEMIS/ALAMY STOCK PHOTO ©

Marina drinks with view of Downtown

happy party people knocking back the brewskis. There's soccer and rugby on the big screen, pool tables, water-sports rentals, a daily happy hour, occasional bands and drink specials on most weeknights. (📞04 318 1313; www.barastibeach. com; King Salman Bin Abdul Aziz Al Saud St, Dubai Media City; admission free; ⏰11am-1.30am Sat-Wed, to 3am Thu & Fri; 🛜; MNakheel)

Lock, Stock & Barrel   BAR

26 🚇 MAP P126, F8

Since opening in 2016, LSB has been racking up the accolades as living proof that there's room in bling-blinded Dubai for keeping-it-real party hangouts. Dressed in industrial chic, this two-level joint is the place for mingling with unpretentious folk over cocktails

and craft beer, the occasional live band and fingerlickin' American soul food. Two-for-one happy hour daily from 4pm to 8pm. (📞04 514 9195; www.lsbdubai.com; 8th fl, Grand Millennium Hotel, Barsha Heights; ⏰4pm-3am Mon-Thu, from 1pm Fri, from 2pm Sat & Sun)

Lucky Voice   KARAOKE

27 🚇 MAP P126, F8

This UK import features private karaoke pods where groups of six to 25 people can belt out tunes from a huge playlist without (much) fear of embarrassment. Even if you're not into singing, come for ladies' nights, Friday brunch or on nights when the house band plays highly danceable funk, rock and soul classics. (📞800 58259; www. luckyvoice.ae; Grand Millennium Hotel,

Barsha Heights; karaoke per hr Dhs50 for first 2 hours, then Dhs30; ⏱4pm-3am; 📶; Ⓜ Dubai Internet City)

Industrial Avenue CLUB

28 🚇 MAP P126, D6

With its graffiti-slathered concrete walls, mismatched furniture and cool electronic tunes, this warehouse-style club tucked behind the China Grill bar channels Shoreditch and Berlin party grit reasonably well. Drinks prices are fair. Be warned: high heels don't do well on the uneven floor. (📞04 511 7139; www.industrialavenuedubai.com; Westin Dubai Mina Seyahi Beach Resort & Marina, King Salman bin Abdulaziz Al Saud St, Dubai Media City; ⏱10pm-3am Thu & Fri)

Jetty Lounge BAR

29 🚇 MAP P126, D6

From the moment you start following the meandering path through One&Only's luxuriant gardens, you'll sense that you're heading for a pretty special place. Classy without the pretence, Jetty Lounge is all about unwinding (preferably at sunset) on plush white sofas scattered right in the sand. There's a full bar menu and global snacks for nibbling. (📞04 399 9999; www.royalmirage.oneandonlyresorts.com; One&Only Royal Mirage, The Palace, King Salman Bin Abdul Aziz Al Saud St, Dubai Media City; ⏱2pm-2am; 📶; Ⓜ Nakheel, 🚊Palm Jumeirah)

Siddharta Lounge BAR

30 🚇 MAP P126, C6

Part of Buddha Bar in the same hotel, Siddharta is an urban oasis and great spot to join Dubai's glam crowd in taking the party from daytime by the pool to basking in the glow of the Marina high-rises. Nice music, expertly mixed cocktails and swift service make up for the rather steep price tab. (📞04 317 6000; www.siddhartalounge.com; Tower 2, Grosvenor House, Al Emreef St, Al Saud St, Dubai Marina; ⏱12.30-3.30pm, 6.30-midnight Sat-Wed, 6pm-12.30am Thu & Fri; 📶; Ⓜ Damac)

Pure Sky Lounge BAR

31 🚇 MAP P126, B6

When it comes to glorious views over The Beach at JBR and Palm Jumeirah, this chic indoor-outdoor lounge is in a lofty league on the 35th floor of the beachfront Hilton. White furniture accented with turquoise pillows channels a chill, maritime mood. (📞04 399 1111; Hilton Dubai Jumeirah, The Walk at JBR, Dubai Marina; ⏱5pm-1am; 📶; Ⓜ Damac, 🚊Jumeirah Beach Residence 1)

Bliss Lounge BAR

32 🚇 MAP P126, A6

Sunset is the perfect time to stake out your turf at the circular bar or on a cushiony sofa in a tented 'pod' at this beachfront lounge with view of the Ain Dubai Ferris wheel. Kick back with a cold one or a *sheesha* while nibbling on sushi and taking in some chill jazz or deep house

Women in the UAE

Some of the biggest misunderstandings between Middle Eastern-ers and people from other parts of the world occur over the issue of women.

Common Misconceptions

Half-truths and stereotypes exist on both sides: foreigners sometimes assume that all Middle Eastern women are veiled, repressed victims, while some locals see Western women as sex-obsessed and immoral.

Many non-Arab people imagine that for women to travel to Dubai is much more difficult and stressful than it is. First up, let's clear up some common myths: You don't have to wear a burka, headscarf or veil. You are allowed to drive a car. You won't be constantly harassed. It's safe to take taxis, stay alone in hotels and walk around on your own in most areas.

Emirati Women in Society

Traditionally, the role of a woman in this region is to be a mother and matron of the household, while the man is the financial provider. However, as with any society, the reality is far more nuanced. Emirati women in the UAE pilot fighter jet planes, work as police officers, undertake research, serve as ambassadors, run corporations and participate in Antarctic exploration. Seven of 29 members of the UAE cabinet are women.

courtesy of a resident DJ. (📞04 315 3886; www.blissloungedubai.com; Sheraton Jumeirah Beach Resort, Al Mamsha St/Te Walk at JBR, Dubai Marina; ⏰12.30pm-2am; 📶; Ⓜ Jumeirah Lakes Towers)

Nasimi Beach BAR

33 🚇 MAP P126, E1

This beach club at the Atlantis caters to hip and libidinous party animals (no kids allowed) working on their tan sprawled on a double sunbed while being showered with house, funk and electro. The vibe picks up in the afternoon, espe-cially on weekends. Happy hour runs from 5pm to 7pm (weekends 6pm to 8pm). (📞04 426 2626; www.atlantistheplan.com; West Beach, Atlantis The Palm, Palm Jumeirah; minimum spend Mon-Thurs Dhs150, Fri-Sun Dhs250; ⏰11am-midnight Sun-Thu, 9am-midnight Fri & Sat; 🚌Aquaventure)

Buddha Bar BAR

34 🚇 MAP P126, C6

Dinner at perennially popular Bud-dha Bar always feels like a special occasion thanks to the theatrical design complete with a 7m-tall

Buddha and the broad-spectrum Asian menu. But this is also a nightlife spot with an upstairs lounge, DJs three nights a week and superb handcrafted cocktails. (📞04 317 6000; www.buddhabar-dubai.com; Grosvenor House, Al Emreef St, Dubai Marina; ⏰7pm-1.30am Sat-Wed, to 2.30am Thu & Fri; 📶; Ⓜ️Damac, � Dubai Marina Mall)

Entertainment

MusicHall
LIVE MUSIC

35 ⭐ MAP P126, C4

It's not a theatre, not a club, not a bar and not a restaurant – but the lavishly designed MusicHall is all those things. The concept hails from Beirut, where it's had audiences clapping since 2003 with an eclectic line-up of 10 live music acts – from Indian to country, and rock to Russian ballads. The food (fusion cuisine and international finger food) is an afterthought. (📞056 270 8670; www.jumeirah.com; ground fl, Jumeirah Zabeel Saray, West Crescent, Palm Jumeirah; mains Dhs170 290, minimum spend Dhs450; ⏰9pm-3am Thu & Fri; 🚌Aquaventure)

Shopping

Dubai Marina Mall
MALL

36 🔒 MAP P126, B7

This mall has an attractive waterfront setting and a manageable 140 stores on four floors, so you won't get lost quite so readily as in its mega-size cousins. Its main architectural feature is the giant atrium where kids can trundle around in a toy train. (📞04 436 1020; www.dubaimarinamall.com; Dubai Marina Walk, Dubai Marina; ⏰10am-11pm Sat-Wed, to midnight Thu & Fri; 📶♿; Ⓜ️Damac)

Gallery One
ART

37 🔒 MAP P126, B6

If you love art but can't afford an original, pick up a highly decorative print by well-known Middle Eastern artists without breaking the bank at this gallery shop. Some motifs are also available as greetings cards, posters, notebooks and calendars. (📞04 423 1987; www.g-1.com; The Walk at JBR, Dubai Marina; ⏰10am-10pm; Ⓜ️Jumeirah Lakes Towers, 🚌Jumeirah Beach Residence 1)

Ginger & Lace
FASHION & ACCESSORIES

38 🔒 MAP P126, A7

This indie shop in Ibn Battuta's India Court stocks an eclectic and rotating selection of colourful, whimsical fashion by high-spirited designers from around the globe. Much of the clothing is rather flashy, so dedicated wallflowers may want to look elsewhere. (📞04 368 5109; www.facebook.com/gingerandlace; Ibn Battuta Mall, Sheikh Zayed Rd, Jebel Ali; ⏰10am-10pm Sun-Wed, to midnight Thu-Sat; Ⓜ️Ibn Battuta)

Dubai Experience 🍽

Let's Do Brunch

*Friday brunch is a major element of the Dubai
social scene and just about every hotel-restaurant
in town sets up an all-you-can-eat buffet with an
option for unlimited wine or bubbly. Some indie
eateries also do brunch but without alcohol. Here
are our top indulgence picks in town. Bookings
are essential.*

Brunch Tips

⊙ Make Friday brunch
reservations at least a
week ahead.

⊙ Head out early –
trying to find a taxi and
battling the traffic at
12:30pm is not fun.

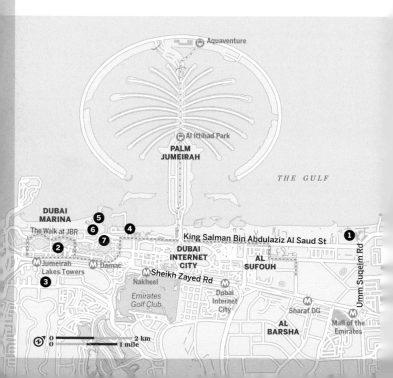

❶ The Motherlode

Expect to loosen your belt after enjoying the cornucopia of delectables at Friday Brunch at **Al Qasr** (www.jumeirah.com; P @ 🛜 🚇; M Mall of the Emirates). Options include barbecued Wagyu burgers and global treats from Bangkok, Paris and Mexico. A live band provides entertainment. Brunch with soft drinks/alcohol Dhs495/595.

❷ Spice Route Brunch

The food is as sumptuous as the decor at **Asia Asia** (p132) restaurant with terrace tables overlooking the Dubai Marina. Work your way from the sushi selection to then feast slow roasted lamb or miso marinated salmon. 2pm to 5pm on Fridays, brunch with soft drinks/champagne Dhs295/Dhs649.

❸ Jazz Brunch

The cheap and cheerful brunch at **Jazz@PizzaExpress** (www.pizzaexpressuae.com; M Jumeirah Lakes Towers) has you filling up on Italian faves ordered à la carte and brought to your table. Live jazz sets the mood. Brunch with/without alcohol Dhs199/129.

❹ International Indulgence

Bubbalicious is the culinary bonanza orchestrated at the **Westin Dubai Mina Seyahi Beach Resort & Marina** (www.westinminaseyahi.com; M Nakheel, 🚇 Mina Seyahi). It also features 10 live cooking stations and family-friendly entertainment such as a petting zoo, Chinese acrobats and a play area. Brunch with soft drinks/sparkling wine/champagne Dhs450/550/680.

❺ Afternoon Revelry

Perfect for sleepyheads, the On-shore Social at the **Zero Gravity** (p134) beach club kicks into gear in the afternoon with avalanche of faves, from dim sum to antipasti and decadent desserts. Stay on for sunset and night-time DJ beats. Brunch costs Dhs395, but if you want sparkling wine and pool and beach access, it's Dhs666.

❻ Fiesta Time

At the Mas Mas Maya brunch by the beach at **Maya Modern Mexican Kitchen** (p133), you can fuel up on fajitas, guacamole and ceviche before finishing with churros and ice cream. Includes pool and beach access to the Royal Meridien Beach Resort & Spa. Brunch is 12.30 to 4pm on Fridays and costs Dhs325/Dhs475 with soft drinks/alcohol.

❼ Carnivorous Delight

Fans of churrasco grills will be in heaven at the Hola Hola brunch at **Toro Toro** (www.torotoro-dubai.com; M Damac, 🚇 Jumeirah Beach Residence 1), a Latin American outpost at the Grosvenor House. This brunch is a great way to sample celebrity chef Richard Sandoval's culinary concoctions. Brunch with/without alcohol costs Dhs380/300.

Worth a Trip 🔭

Abu Dhabi

The first Louvre outside France, an ethereally beautiful mosque, the world's fastest roller coaster, a head-spinning Formula One racetrack. About 150km south of Dubai, the UAE capital Abu Dhabi may not be quite as flashy as its northern cousin but – almost stealthily – it has built an impressive portfolio of attractions and sharpened its profile as a popular tourist destination of its own. Welcome to an exciting city where nothing stands still.

Abu Dhabi is a simple day trip from Dubai, easily manageable on public transport or by yourself.

🚌 Every 40 minutes from Dubai's Al Gubaiba station in Bur Dubai (single/return Dhs25/40, two hours)

🚗 Taxis cost around Dhs300.

Louvre Abu Dhabi

The stunning Jean Nouvel–designed **Louvre Abu Dhabi** (http://louvreabudhabi.ae; Cultural District, Saadiyat Island; Dhs60) finally opened in late 2017. Sunlight filters through its huge perforated dome onto a cluster of 23 galleries sheltering 600 priceless works that illustrate our shared humanity across time, ethnicity and geography. Highlights include a Da Vinci painting, a Chinese Buddha and a bronze from Benin.

Sheikh Zayed Grand Mosque

Rising majestically from beautifully manicured gardens, the **Sheikh Zayed Grand Mosque** (pictured; www.szgmc.ae; off Sheikh Rashid Bin Saeed St; admission free; ⏰9am-10pm Sat-Thu, 4.30-10pm Fri, tours 10am, 11am, 2pm, 5pm & 7pm Sun-Thu, 5pm & 7pm Fri) represents an impressive welcome to the city. It accommodates 50,000 worshippers and is one of the few in the region open to non-Muslims.

Emirates Palace

What the Burj Khalifa in Dubai is to the vertical, the **Emirates Palace** (www.emiratespalace.com; Corniche Rd (West); admission free) is to the horizontal, with audacious domed gatehouses and flying ramps to the foyer, 114 domes and a 1.3km private beach. Built for Dhs11 billion, this is the big hotel in the Gulf, with 1002 crystal chandeliers and 392 luxury rooms and suites.

Abu Dhabi Falcon Hospital

Falcons are an integral part of traditional Gulf culture, which is what makes this **facility** (www.falconhospital.com; Sweihan Rd; 2hr tour adult/child Dhs170/60; ⏰tours 2pm Sat, 10am & 2pm Sun-Thu) much-needed and much-loved. Tours include visits to the falcon museum, the examination room and the free-flight aviary. Reservations required.

★ Top Tips

o To get your bearings, consider a trip on the hop-on, hop-off **Big Bus Abu Dhabi** (📞02 449 0026; www.bigbustours.com; 24hr adult/child Dhs255/166, 48hr adult/child Dhs299/192; ⏰9am-5pm).

o Take a free guided tour of the Grand Mosque, which includes a Q&A (in English).

✕ Take a Break

Al Dhafra (www.aldhafrauae.ae; Al Mina Port; buffet lunch/dinner from Dhs120/99, dinner cruise Dhs150; ⏰noon-5pm & 6.30-11.15pm; 📞) is a hidden Arab gem serving the best Emirati cuisine in town.

For the ultimate indulgence, order a cappuccino sprinkled with 24-karat gold flakes (Dhs60) at **Le Café** (www.emiratespalace.com; Corniche Rd (West), Emirates Palace; high tea Dhs380-480; ⏰high tea 2-6pm; 📞) in the Emirates Palace

Survival Guide

Abra (wooden ferry) on Dubai Creek CLARI MASSIMILIANO/SHUTTERSTOCK ©

Before You Go

Book Your Stay

o Room rates fluctuate enormously, spiking during festivals, holidays and big events and dropping in the summer months.

o A 10% municipal tax, 10% service fee, 5% VAT and a 'tourism tax' ranging from Dh7 to Dh20 per night are added to room rates.

o Even midrange hotels often have superb facilities, including a pool, multiple restaurants, a gym, satellite TV and a bar.

o Not all hotels are licensed to serve alcohol, so check if this is important to you.

o Hotel apartments are great for self-caterers, families and groups.

o Nostalgic types should check into the growing crop of heritage boutique hotels in Bur Dubai and Deira.

o By law, unmarried men and women are not permitted to share a room, but in reality

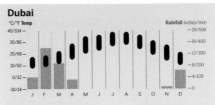

When to Go

o **Winter (Dec–Feb)** Moderate temperatures, short days, occasional rain, many festivals and activities.

o **Spring (Mar–Apr)** Perfect beach weather with temperatures around 30°C.

o **Summer (Jul–Sep)** Temperatures soar (to an average 43°C with stifling 95% humidity), hotel rates drop.

o **Autumn (Oct–Nov)** Warm weather, balmy nights, life moves back outdoors.

most hotels turn a blind eye.

o Free wi-fi is commonplace, with only a few hotels charging as much Dhs100 per day for access.

Useful Websites

Lonely Planet (www.lonelyplanet.com/united-arab-emirates/dubai/hotels) Recommendations and bookings.

Visit Dubai (www.visitdubai.com) The official tourist authority site also has accommodation-booking function.

Dnata (www.dnata travel.com) Major travel agency for the Middle Eastern market, based in Dubai.

Best Budget

Rove Downtown (www.rovehotels.com) Budget-friendly urban base with Burj Khalifa views.

Ibis Mall of the Emirates (www.ibis.com) Predictably basic but comfortable and in a primo location.

Premier Inn Dubai International Airport (https://global.premierinn.com)

Easy in, easy out at this airport-adjacent budget designer hotel.

Rove City Centre (www.rovehotels.com) Hip yet down-to-earth with amenities more typical of posher players.

Centro Barsha (www.rotana.com/centro-barsha) Designer hotel with key lifestyle and tech touches near Mall of the Emirates.

Best Midrange

XVA Hotel (www.xvahotel.com) Connect to the magic of a bygone era in this art-filled heritage den.

Le Meridien Mina Seyahi Beach Resort (www.lemeridien-minaseyahi.com) Good-value waterfront outpost for sporty types.

Media One Hotel (www.mediaonehotel.com) High-octane hot spot with mod design, party pedigree and unpretentious attitude.

Pearl Marina Hotel Apartments (www.pearlmarinahotel.com) All the charms of Dubai Marina at your feet without hav-

ing to rob a bank.

Beach Hotel Apartment (http://beachhotelapartment.ae) Rare bargain in Jumeirah with a killer location and easy access to tanning and shopping.

Best Top End

Al Qasr Hotel (www.jumeirah.com) Posh player with A-lister clientele, 2km of private beach and canalside dining.

Grosvenor House (www.grosvenor-house-dubai.com) Art deco–inspired hotel draws local trend-chasers to its hip bars and restaurants.

One&Only The Palm (http://thepalm.oneandonlyresorts.com) Sumptuous resort with Moorish-style design accents, lavish Arabian-style and expansive gardens.

Park Hyatt Dubai Class act surrounded by lush landscaping with superb facilities and golf course access.

Raffles Dubai (www.raffles.com/dubai) Slick, chic decor with water features and

top-rated Japanese rooftop restaurant and lounge.

Palace Downtown (www.theaddress.com) Romantic inner-city pad with easy access to top shopping and dreamy views of Burj Khalifa.

Arriving in Dubai

Dubai International Airport

o Most international flights land at this airport north of Deira.

o Dubai metro's Red Line runs from 5.30am to midnight (to 1am Thursday and Friday) from terminals 1 and 3. On Fridays, train service starts at 10am.

o Up to two pieces of luggage are permitted.

o A travel pass called 'Nol card' must be purchased at the station.

o Taxis wait outside each arrivals terminal 24/7. A surcharge of Dhs25 applies to rides originating at the airport, plus Dhs1.96 per kilometre.

Nol Cards

○ Travel on public transport requires the purchase of a Nol ticket or card at ticket stations or from vending machines before boarding.

○ Cards must be tapped onto the card reader upon entering and exiting at which point the correct fare will be deducted.

○ Short-term visitors should get the Nol Red Ticket, which costs Dh2 plus credit for at least one trip, and can be recharged up to 10 times; may only be used on a single mode of transport at a time.

○ If you intend to make more than 10 trips, get the prepaid Nol Silver Card (Dhs25, including Dhs19 credit).

○ For full details, see www.nol.ae.

○ Approximate taxi fares are Dhs50 to Deira, Dhs60 to Bur Dubai, Dhs70 to Downtown Dubai, Dhs110 to Madinat Jumeirah and Dhs130 to Dubai Marina.

Al Maktoum International Airport

○ Dubai's new airport is a work in progress about 50km south of Downtown and receives limited flights.

○ Bus F55 links the airport with the Ibn Battuta metro station hourly. From here, the Red Line serves most key districts.

○ Taxis wait outside the passenger terminal. Approximate fares are Dhs70 to Dubai Marina, Dhs110 to Downtown Dubai and Dhs120 to Bur Dubai.

Getting Around

Metro

○ Dubai metro operates two lines. The Red Line links Rashidiya near Dubai International Airport with Jebel Ali past Dubai Marina, handily parallel to Sheikh Zayed Rd. The Green Line links Etisalat with Creek station near Dubai Healthcare City.

○ Trains run roughly every 10 minutes from 5am to midnight Saturday to Wednesday, to 1am Thursday, and from 10am to 1am on Friday.

○ Fares range from from Dhs2 to Dhs6.50.

○ For details and trip planning visit www.wojhati.rta.ae.

Taxi

○ Taxis can be hailed in the street, picked up at taxi ranks or booked by phone.

○ Flagfall for street taxis: Dhs8 between 6am and 10pm; Dhs9 between 10pm and 6am. Drivers accept credit cards.

○ The per kilometre fare is Dhs1.82, with a minimum fare of Dhs12.

○ Destinations are generally not given via a street address but by mentioning the nearest landmark (eg a hotel, mall, roundabout, major building).

Boat

o Abras (traditional wooden boats; Dh1) are a wonderful way to cross the Creek between Bur Dubai and Deira.

o Water buses (Dh3 to Dh5 per trip) are air-conditioned and link four stops around the Dubai Marina.

o Dubai Ferry (Dh50; www.dubai-ferry.com) operates between Dubai Marina and Bur Dubai and along the Dubai Canal. Both routes interlink at Dubai Canal station.

Bus

o Buses are clean, comfortable, air-conditioned and cheap, but they're slow and commuter geared.

o Fares range from Dhs3 to Dhs8.50 and Nol Cards must be used.

o For information, check http://dubai-buses.com; for trip planning, go to www.wojhati.rta.ae.

Essential Information

Business Hours

Restaurants noon-3pm and 7.30pm-midnight.

Shopping malls 10am-10pm Sunday to Wednesday, 10am-midnight Thursday to Saturday.

Souqs 9am-1pm and 4pm-9pm Saturday to Thursday, 4pm-9pm Friday.

Electricity

Type G
230V/50Hz

LGBT Travellers

o Homosexual acts are illegal under UAE law and can incur a jail term and fines.

o If you see Arab men walking hand in hand, it's a sign of friendship and not an indication of sexual orientation.

o Public displays of affection between partners are taboo regardless of sexual orientation.

o Sharing a room is likely to be construed as companionable or cost-cutting but being discreet about your true relationship is advisable.

Money

o The UAE dirham (Dh) is pegged to the US dollar. One dirham is divided into 100 fils.

o ATMs are widely available. Credit cards are accepted in most hotels, restaurants and shops.

o Exchange offices tend to offer better rates than banks. Reliable outlets include UAE Exchange or Al Rostamani, both with multiple branches in shopping malls and around town.

Money-Saving Tips

o Most museums and galleries are either free or charge just a few dirham for admission.

o Top attractions such as the Dubai Fountains, the souqs and the Creek waterfront are also free.

o Take advantage of deals on drinks and nibbles during happy hours and ladies' nights.

o Travel on the Dubai metro for longer distances and use a taxi to get to your final destination from the nearest station.

o Fuel up for pocket change on curries, kebabs, shwarma, samosas, dosas, momos and other exotic and delicious delectables brought to Dubai by its global expats.

o Check out top thoroughbreds or gangly dromedaries at highly popular horse and camel races – admission is free.

o If you can stand the heat, visit in July or August when hotel prices plummet.

Tipping

o Tip porters and room cleaners Dhs5 to Dhs10 per day. Waiters and spa staff get 10% to 15% of the bill (in cash). In taxis round up to the nearest note.

Safe Travel

o Using illegal drugs in Dubai is considered a crime and simply a bad, bad idea.

o There's a zero-tolerance policy on drinking and driving (0% is the blood-alcohol limit).

o The import of certain prescription medicines is restricted unless you can present an original prescription and a letter from your doctor confirming that you need to take it. See www.uaeinteract.com/travel/drug.asp for an overview.

o If you have an accident, even a small one, you must call the police (☏999) and wait at the scene. If it's a minor accident, move your car to the side of the road. You cannot file an insurance claim without a police report.

o Dubai is a safe city for women and it's fine to take cabs and walk around on your own. Modest dress is recommended but there's no need to cover up.

o Water hazards The Gulf may look innocuous, but rip currents can be very strong and drownings occur regularly.

Toilets

o Public toilets in shopping centres, museums, restaurants and hotels are Western style, free and generally clean and well maintained.

Islamic Holidays

Islamic Year	Ramadan	Eid al Fitr	Eid al Adha
1436 (2018)	16 May	14 Jun	21 Aug
1437 (2019)	6 May	4 Jun	11 Aug
1438 (2020)	24 Apr	23 May	30 Jul
1439 (2021)	13 Apr	13 May	20 Jul

○ The hose next to the toilet is used for rinsing (left hand only if you want to go native); toilet paper is used for drying only and should be thrown in the bin to avoid clogging the toilets

Tourist Information

The **Dubai Department of Tourism & Commerce Marketing** (☏ 600 555 559; www.visit dubai.com; ☻ 8am-8pm Sat-Thu) has no brick and-mortar office but does maintain a comprehensive website and a call centre for information on hotels, attractions, shopping and other topics.

Travellers with Disabilities

○ Most buildings are wheelchair-accessible, but drop-down curbs are still rare and practically non-existent in Bur Dubai and Deira.

○ Dubai's metro has lifts and grooved guidance paths in stations and wheelchair spaces in each train compartment.

Dos & Don'ts

○ Do ask before taking a photo of locals.

○ Do remove your shoes before entering an Emirati home.

○ Do wear swimwear only by the pool or on the beach.

○ Do accept any hospitality offered; for example, coffee or dates.

○ Don't swear, shout or make offensive gestures (giving the finger, sticking out your tongue etc).

○ Don't get drunk in public places as it may lead to fines or possibly jail time.

○ Don't point your finger or the soles of your feet towards locals.

○ Don't indulge in public displays of affection (holding hands is OK).

○ International chains and all top-end hotels have rooms with extra-wide doors and adapted bathrooms.

○ Shopping malls are accessible, as are most bars and restaurants.

○ Some beaches, including Kite Beach and Sunset Beach, have boardwalks leading through the sand to the waterfront.

Visas

○ Citizens of 49 countries, including all EU countries, the US, the UK, Canada and Australia, are eligible for free 30-day single-entry visas on arrival in Dubai.

○ Travellers not eligible for an on-arrival visa (including transit visitors) must have a visitor visa arranged through a sponsor, such as your Dubai hotel, a tour operator or a relative or friend in Dubai before arriving.

○ Entry requirements to the UAE are in constant flux. Always obtain the latest requirements from the UAE embassy in your home country.

Language

MSA (Modern Standard Arabic) –
the official lingua franca of the Arab
world – and the everyday spoken
version are quite different. The
Arabic variety spoken in Dubai (and
provided in this chapter) is known
as Gulf Arabic.

Note that *gh* is a throaty sound
(like the French 'r'), *r* is rolled, *dh*
is pronounced as the 'th' in 'that',
th as in 'thin', *ch* as in 'cheat' and
kh as the 'ch' in the Scottish *loch*.
The apostrophe (') indicates the
glottal stop (like the pause in the
middle of 'uh-oh'). Bearing these
points in mind and reading our pro-
nunciation guides as if they were
English, you'll be understood. The
stressed syllables are indicated
with italics. The markers (m) and
(f) indicate masculine and feminine
word forms respectively.

To enhance your trip with a
phrasebook, visit **lonelyplanet.com**.
Lonely Planet iPhone phrasebooks
are available through the Apple
App store.

Basics

Hello.
اهلا و سهلا.   *ah·lan was ah·lan*

Goodbye.
مع السلامة.   *ma' sa·laa·ma*

Yes./No.
نعم./لا.   *na·'am/la*

Please.
من فضلك.   *min fad·lak* (m)
من فضلك.   *min fad·lik* (f)

Thank you.
شكران.   *shuk·ran*

Excuse me.
اسمح لي.   *is·mah lee* (m)
اسمحي لي.   *is·mah·ee lee* (f)

Sorry.
مع الأسف.   *ma' al·as·af*

Do you speak English?
تتكلم/تتكلمي   *tit·kal·am/tit·ka·la·mee*
انجليزية؟   *in·glee·zee·ya* (m/f)

I don't understand.
مو فاهم.   *moo faa·him*

Eating & Drinking

I'd like (the) ..., please.
عطني/عطيني   *a·ti·nee/'a·tee·nee*
الـ ... من فضلك.   *il ... min fad·lak* (m/f)

  bill   قائمة   *kaa·'i·ma*

  drink list   قائم   *kaa·'i·mat*
     المشروبات   *il·mash·roo·baat*

  menu   الطعام   *kaa·'i·mat*
     قائمة   *i·ta·'aam*

  that dish   الطبق   *i·tab·ak*
     هاذاك   *haa·dhaa·ka*

What would you recommend?
اش تنصح؟   *aash tan·sah* (m)
اش تنصحي؟   *aash tan·sa·hee* (f)

Do you have vegetarian food?
عندك طعم   *'an·dak ta·'am*
نباتي؟   *na·baa·tee*

Shopping

I'm looking for ...
مدور على ...   *moo·daw·ir 'a·la ...* (m)
مدورة على ...   *moo·daw·i·ra 'a·la ...* (f)

Can I look at it?
ممكن اشوف؟   *mum·kin a·shoof*

How much is it? بكم؟   *bi·kam*

That's too expensive.
غالي جداً.   *ghaa·lee jid·an*

What's your lowest price?
اش السعر الاخر؟   *aash i·si'r il·aa·khir*

Do you have any others?
عندك اخرين؟   *'and·ak ukh·reen* (m)
عندك اخرين؟   *'and·ik ukh·reen* (f)

Emergencies

Help!
مساعد!   *moo·saa·'id* (m)
مساعدة!   *moo·saa·'id·a* (f)

Call a doctor!
تصل/تصلي   *ti·sil/ti·si·lee*
على طبيب!   *'a·la ta·beeb* (m/f)

Call the police!
تصل/تصلي   *ti·sil/ti·si·lee*
على الشرطة!   *'a·la i·shur·ta* (m/f)

I'm lost.
انا ضعت.   *a·na duht*

I'm sick.
انا مريض.   *a·na ma·reed* (m)
انا مريضة.   *a·na ma·ree·da* (f)

Where are the toilets?
وين المرحاض؟   *wayn il·mir·haad*

Time & Numbers

What time is it?/At what time?
الساعة كم؟   *i·saa·a' kam*

It's/At (two) o'clock.
الساعة (ثنتين).   *i·saa·a' (thin·tayn)*

yesterday ... البارح ...   *il·baa·rih ...*

tomorrow ... باكر ...   *baa·chir ...*

  morning صباح   *sa·baah*

  afternoon بعد الظهر   *ba'd a·thuhr*

  evening مساء   *mi·saa*

1	١	واحد	*waa·hid*
2	٢	اثنين	*ith·nayn*
3	٣	ثلاثة	*tha·laa·tha*
4	٤	اربع	*ar·ba'*
5	٥	خمسة	*kham·sa*
6	٦	ستة	*si·ta*
7	٧	سبعة	*sa·ba'*
8	٨	ثمانية	*tha·maan·ya*
9	٩	تسعة	*tis·a'*
10	١٠	عشرة	*'ash·ar·a*
100	١٠٠	مية	*mee·ya*
1000	١٠٠٠	الف	*alf*

Transport & Directions

Where's the ...?
من وين ...؟   *min wayn ...*

What's the address?
ما العنوان؟   *ma il·'un·waan*

Can you show me (on the map)?
لو سمحت   *law sa·maht*
وريني   *wa·ree·nee*
(علخريطة)؟   *('al·kha·ree·ta)*

How far is it?
كم بعيد؟   *kam ba·'eed*

Please take me to (this address).
من فضلك خذني   *min fad·lak khudh·nee*
(علعنوان هاذا).   *('al·'un·waan haa·dha)*

Please stop here.
لو سمحت   *law sa·maht*
وقف هنا.   *wa·gif hi·na*

What time's the bus?
الساعة كم   *a·saa·a' kam*
الباص؟   *il·baas*

What station/ stop is this?
ما هي   *maa hee·ya*
المحطة هاذي؟   *il·ma·ha·ta haa·dhee*

Index

See also separate subindexes for:

⊗ Eating p156
⊕ Drinking p157
✪ Entertainment p157
🔒 Shopping p158

Sights 000
Map Pages **000**

Behind the Scenes

Send Us Your Feedback

We love to hear from travellers – your comments help make our books better. We read every word, and we guarantee that your feedback goes straight to the authors. Visit **lonelyplanet.com/contact** to submit your updates and suggestions.

Note: We may edit, reproduce and incorporate your comments in Lonely Planet products such as guidebooks, websites and digital products, so let us know if you don't want your comments reproduced or your name acknowledged. For a copy of our privacy policy visit lonelyplanet.com/privacy.

Andrea's Thanks

Heartfelt thanks to all the wonderful people who so graciously and generously supplied me with insider tips, background info and insights to make my Dubai research fun and fruitful, including: Rashi, Abhi & Mia Sen, Arva Ahmed, Regine Schneider, Patricia Liebscher, Christian Sanger, Dara Toulch, Janeen Mansour, Paul Matthews, Dominic Ritzer, Sameer Dasouqi, Julia Alvaro and Katie Roberts.

Kevin's Thanks

Thanks to my wife, Adriana Schmidt Raub, who joined for a few days and fell unexpectedly in love with Abu Dhabi! Lauren Keith, Andrea Schulte-Peevers and all at LP. On the road, Rauda Al Falasi, Alya Al Nuaimi, Paul Oliver, Paula Carreiro, Amer Ghussein, Monique Safayan, Rianne Norbart, Ayan Alieva, Arianna Posenato, Saeed Suleiman, Sam Ioannidis and Hamad Ghanem Shaheen AlGhanem.

Acknowledgements

Cover photograph: View of Burj Khalifa from Waterfront Promenade, Massimo Borchi/4Corners ©

Photographs pp26–7 (from left): Seqoya; Tasfotonl; Fedor Selivanov/ Shutterstock ©

This Book

This 5th edition of Lonely Planet's *Pocket Dubai* guidebook was researched and written by Andrea Schulte-Peevers and Kevin Raub. The previous edition was written by Andrea Schulte-Peevers. This guidebook was produced by the following:

Destination Editor
Lauren Keith

Series Designer
Campbell McKenzie

Cartographic Series Designer
Wayne Murphy

Product Editor
Shona Gray

Senior Cartographer
Valentina Kremenchutskaya

Book Designer
Meri Blazevski

Assisting Editors
Imogen Bannister, Kellie Langdon, Jodie Martire, Kate Morgan

Cover Researcher
Wibowo Rusli

Thanks to Lara Brunt, Liz Heynes, Bart Hoffmann, Georg Jenichl, Clara Monitto, Lindsey Parry, Martine Power, Rachel Rawling, Kirsten Rawlings

Our Writers

Andrea Schulte-Peevers

Born and raised in Germany and educated in London and at UCLA, Andrea has travelled the distance to the moon and back in her visits to some 75 countries. She has earned her living as a professional travel writer for over two decades and authored or contributed to nearly 100 Lonely Planet titles as well as to newspapers, magazines and websites around the world. She also works as a travel consultant, translator and editor. She makes her home in Berlin. Follow Andrea on Twitter @ASchultePeevers.

Kevin Raub

Atlanta native Kevin Raub started his career as a music journalist in New York, working for *Men's Journal* and *Rolling Stone* magazines. He ditched the rock 'n' roll lifestyle for travel writing and has written nearly 50 Lonely Planet guides, focused mainly on Brazil, Chile, Colombia, USA, India, the Caribbean and Portugal. Raub also contributes to a variety of travel magazines in both the USA and UK. Along the way, the self-confessed hophead is in constant search of wildly high IBUs in local beers. Follow him on Twitter and Instagram @RaubOnTheRoad.

Published by Lonely Planet Global Limited
CRN 554153
5th edition – Dec 2018
ISBN 978 1 78657 073 4
© Lonely Planet 2018   Photographs © as indicated 2018
10 9 8 7 6 5 4 3 2 1
Printed in Singapore